WRITING
essentials

for the Pre-GED Student

Laurie Rozakis, Ph.D.

THOMSON

ARCO

Australia • Canada • Mexico • Singapore • Spain • United Kingdom • United States

An ARCO Book

ARCO is a registered trademark of Thomson Learning, Inc., and is used herein under license by Peterson's.

About The Thomson Corporation and Peterson's

The Thomson Corporation, with 2002 revenues of $7.8 billion, is a global leader in providing integrated information solutions to business and professional customers. The Corporation's common shares are listed on the Toronto and New York stock exchanges (TSX: TOC; NYSE: TOC). Its learning businesses and brands serve the needs of individuals, learning institutions, corporations, and government agencies with products and services for both traditional and distributed learning. Peterson's (www.petersons.com) is a leading provider of education information and advice, with books and online resources focusing on education search, test preparation, and financial aid. Its Web site offers searchable databases and interactive tools for contacting educational institutions, online practice tests and instruction, and planning tools for securing financial aid. Peterson's serves 110 million education consumers annually.

For more information, contact Peterson's, 2000 Lenox Drive, Lawrenceville, NJ 08648; 800-338-3282; or find us on the World Wide Web at: www.petersons.com/about

ISBN: 0-7689-1252-0

Printed in the United States of America

10 9 8 7 6 5 4 3 2 1   05 04 03

First Edition

Contents

Introduction   v

Section I   Evaluating Your Skills

Pretest   3

Section II   Organization

1 Topic Sentences   11

2 Unity and Coherence   19

Section III   Sentence Structure

3 Sentence Fragments   29

4 Coordination and Subordination   39

5 Dangling and Misplaced Modifiers   49

6 Parallel Structure   59

Section IV   Usage

7 Subject-Verb Agreement   71

8 Verb Tense   83

Section V   Mechanics

9 Capitalization   95

10 Punctuation   105

11 Contractions and Possessive Pronouns   115

Section VI   The Language Arts, Writing Test

12 The Writing Process   127

13 Patterns of Organization   137

14 Using Specific Details   149

15 Revising and Proofreading   157

Section VII   Reevaluating Your Skills

Posttest   169

Section VIII   Appendices

A Sample Essays   187

B Essay Evaluation Guide   203

C About the GED   205

Introduction

You have taken a big step toward success on the GED Language Arts, Writing Test by using this book. We know that you have a full, busy life and need a test-prep book that gives you fast and easy access to the skills that you need. We have created *Writing Essentials for the Pre-GED Student* with that in mind.

How to Study Writing

- Read all the chapters in this book in order from the beginning to the end.

- Do all the exercises.

- Score yourself, using the answer key.

- Review any chapters that you found confusing. Do the exercises again.

- Write all the essays. Use the checklist to help you assess your work.

About This Book

First, you're going to take the Pretest. The Pretest will help you figure out which sections of the book you'll need to focus on. The book is then divided into five review sections:

1. Organization

2. Sentence Structure

3. Usage

4. Mechanics

5. The Writing Test

By studying these sections, you will learn the writing skills that you need to take the GED, including:

- Writing great topic sentences
- Understanding subject-verb agreement
- Following grammar rules
- Writing with meaning
- Revising and proofreading your essay

You'll also work with practice writing drills in these review sections. The answers to these "Quick Quizzes" are located at the end of each capter, before the practice tests. After the review sections, you'll take the Posttest to see how much you have learned. Finally, we have included some test-taking tips and strategies in the appendix to help you on test day.

By the time we're finished, you'll be confident in your writing abilities.

About the GED Language Arts, Writing Test

The first part of the test has 50 multiple-choice questions that ask you to correct errors in grammar, usage, mechanics, sentence structure, and unity. To help you get ready to prepare for the GED, we begin with the basics. We'll start off slowly and help you along the way. Here is a chart that shows you how the test is organized:

Test	Content	Items	Time Limit
Language Arts, Writing, Part I	Multiple-choice	50 questions	75 minutes
Language Arts, Writing, Part II	Essay	1	45 minutes

You must take both parts of the test, the multiple-choice questions and the essay. The scores you earn on both parts are combined, and they are reported as one score.

Let's get started.

Evaluating Your Skills

Pretest

Directions: Choose the one best answer to each question.

Questions 1–10 refer to the following paragraph:

(1) Our mission at Lake Whisper is to educate visitors about the National Park ecosystem and inspiring travelers to visit the park. (2) Through intensive and innovative classes and hands-on seminars. (3) Mountain ranges are also part of the vast National Parks system, supported by your tax dollars. (4) Visiting instructors emphasizes learning through adventurous hands-on exploration. (5) Providing custom workshops for individuals, small groups, or classes is our "Explore Lake Whisper" program. (6) Your group is looking for an ecology workshop at a time when we don't offer one. (7) We will do our best to arrange one. (8) We offer outdoor education programs for adults that take place at the Pine Barrens and Cove Beach. (9) Some of are classes are indoors, but there always held on rainy days. (10) Participants in recent classes saw wild birds build nests and looks at turtles laying eggs.

1. Sentence 1: **Our mission at Lake Whisper is to educate visitors about the National Park ecosystem and <u>inspiring travelers</u> to visit the parks.**

    Which is the best way to write the underlined portion of this sentence?

    (1) No change

    (2) to inspire travelers

    (3) having travelers be inspired

    (4) travelers being inspired

    (5) travelers be inspired

3

2. Sentence 2: **Through intensive and innovative classes and hands-on seminars.**

   Which correction should be made to sentence 2?

   (1) Replace <u>through</u> with <u>by</u>

   (2) Remove <u>through</u>

   (3) Replace the second <u>and</u> with a comma

   (4) Add a semicolon after <u>classes</u>

   (5) Add this sentence to the end of sentence 1

3. Sentence 3: **Mountain ranges are also part of the vast National Parks system, supported by your tax dollars.**

   Which revision should be made to the placement of sentence 3?

   (1) Place it before sentence 1

   (2) Place it before sentence 2

   (3) Place it before sentence 5

   (4) Place it before sentence 6

   (5) Delete it because it is off the topic

4. Sentence 4: **Visiting <u>instructors emphasizes</u> learning through adventurous hands-on exploration.**

   Which correction should be made to the underlined portion of sentence 4?

   (1) instructors emphasize

   (2) instructors emphasizing

   (3) instructors emphasized

   (4) instructors have emphasized

   (5) instructors do emphasizes

5. Sentence 5: **Providing custom workshops for individuals, small groups, or classes is our "Explore Lake Whisper" program.**

   The most effective revision of sentence 5 would begin with which group of words?

   (1) Having provided custom workshops for individuals, small groups, or classes is our "Explore Lake Whisper" program.

   (2) Our "Explore Lake Whisper" program provides custom workshops for individuals, small groups, or classes.

   (3) To provide custom workshops for individuals, small groups, or classes is our "Explore Lake Whisper" program.

   (4) Being able to provide custom workshops for individuals, small groups, or classes is our "Explore Lake Whisper" program.

   (5) Our "Explore Lake Whisper" program providing custom workshops for individuals, small groups, or classes.

6. Sentences 6 and 7: **Your group is looking for an ecology workshop at a time when we don't offer one. We will do our best to arrange one.**

    What is the best way to combine these sentences?

    (1) Your group is looking for an ecology workshop at a time when we don't offer one, we will do our best to arrange one.

    (2) Your group is looking for an ecology workshop at a time when we don't offer one because we will do our best to arrange one.

    (3) Although your group is looking for an ecology workshop at a time when we don't offer one, we will do our best to arrange one.

    (4) We will do our best to arrange one if your group is looking for an ecology workshop at a time when we don't offer one.

    (5) If your group is looking for an ecology workshop at a time when we don't offer one, we will do our best to arrange one.

7. Sentence 8: **We offer outdoor education programs for adults that take place at the Pine Barrens and Cove Beach.**

    Which correction should be made to sentence 8?

    (1) That take place at the Pine Barrens and Cove Beach, we offer adult outdoor education programs.

    (2) We offer adult outdoor education programs that takes place at the Pine Barrens and Cove Beach.

    (3) Offering adult outdoor education programs that take place at the Pine Barrens and Cove Beach.

    (4) Taking place at the Pine Barrens and Cove Beach, we offer adult outdoor education programs.

    (5) We offer adult outdoor education programs that take place at the Pine Barrens and Cove Beach.

8. Sentence 9: **Some of are classes are indoors, but there always held on rainy days.**

    Which correction(s) should be made to sentence 9?

    (1) Change <u>are</u> to <u>our</u>

    (2) Change <u>there</u> to <u>they're</u>

    (3) Change <u>are</u> to <u>our</u> and change <u>there</u> to <u>they're</u>

    (4) Change <u>there</u> to <u>their</u>

    (5) Change <u>held</u> to <u>helds</u> and change <u>there</u> to <u>their</u>

9. Sentence 10: **Participants in recent classes saw wild birds build nests and looks at turtles laying eggs.**

Which correction should be made to sentence 10?

(1) Participants in recent classes saw wild birds build nests and looking at turtles laying eggs.

(2) Participants in recent classes saw wild birds build nests and were looking at turtles laying eggs.

(3) Participants in recent classes saw wild birds build nests looks at turtles laying eggs.

(4) Participants in recent classes saw wild birds build nests and looked at turtles laying eggs.

(5) Participants in recent classes seeing wild birds build nests and looking at turtles laying eggs.

10. Which sentence best concludes this passage?

(1) Our instructors are highly trained in nature studies.

(2) You will learn a lot and enjoy nature at our Lake Whisper programs.

(3) People also saw condors, a protected species.

(4) We are a field institute.

(5) Recent classes helped participants find ancient artifacts.

Essay

Directions: At the end of this book or on a separate sheet of paper, write an essay about the topic given below. Be sure to revise and proofread your essay.

Suppose you had the opportunity to travel anywhere in the world. Explain where you would travel and why. Use your personal observations, experience, and knowledge to support your ideas.

Answers

1. **The correct answer is (2).** *Parallel words* share the same part of speech. They can all be nouns, adjectives, or verbs, for example. The words must also be in the same tense (if they are verbs). In this sentence, "to inspire" parallels "to educate" because both are in the base form of the verb. See Chapter 6 to review parallel structure.

2. **The correct answer is (5).** Sentence 2 is a *fragment,* and it must be added to a complete sentence to be correct and state the author's ideas. See Chapters 3 and 4 to review sentence structure.

3. **The correct answer is (5).** This sentence is off the topic and should, therefore, be cut. See Chapter 2 to review unity and coherence.

4. **The correct answer is (1).** *Agreement* is all about matching the subject and verb. When subjects and verbs agree, your sentences sound smooth and correct. The plural subject "instructors" requires the plural verb "emphasize." See Chapter 7 to review subject-verb agreement.

5. **The correct answer is (2).** The sentence that makes the most sense is: *Our "Explore Lake Whisper" program provides custom workshops for individuals, small groups, or classes.* See Chapters 3 and 4 to review sentence structure.

6. **The correct answer is (5).** Make the first clause—"Your group is looking for an ecology workshop at a time when we don't offer one"—the *dependent* clause. Make the second clause—"We will do our best to arrange one."—the *main* clause. Use the conjunction "if" to join the two clauses. This links the ideas together and makes the most sense. See Chapters 3 and 4 to review sentence structure.

7. **The correct answer is (5).** As written, this sentence states that the adults, not the outdoor education programs, take place at the Pine Barrens and Cove Beach. This is called a *misplaced modifier.* See Chapter 5 to review this writing error.

8. **The correct answer is (3).** "Our" is needed here to show that something is owned. "They're" means *they are;* this is the contraction that the sentence needs. Review Chapter 11 for help with confusing word pairs.

9. **The correct answer is (4).** Do not switch tenses in the middle of a sentence or passage. The sentence begins in the past tense ("saw"), and so it must continue in that tense ("looked"). See Chapter 8 to review how to use consistent verb tense.

10. **The correct answer is (2).** This sentence repeats the topic sentence and the main ideas in this paragraph. The words "learn a lot" are another way of saying "to educate." The words "enjoy nature" are another way of saying "inspire travelers." See Chapter 1 to review topic sentences and Chapter 2 to review unity and coherence.

Ways to Assess Your Essay

After you write your essay, ask a teacher or someone whose writing you admire to use this checklist to assess your essay. You will also use this checklist to assess the essays that you will write later on in this book.

1. **Main Ideas**

   _____ Do my main points directly answer the question?

   _____ Are my main points persuasive and logical? Will they convince my readers that my point is valid?

   _____ Are my ideas linked in a logical way? Does my essay have unity?

2. **Organization**

   _____ Does my essay have a clear beginning that introduces my main points?

   _____ Does my essay have at least two body paragraphs? Do I start a new paragraph for each main point?

   _____ Does my essay have a conclusion that sums up my main points?

3. **Development of Ideas**

   _____ Do I include specific details to make my point? (*Details* are examples, facts, statistics, reasons, definitions, and descriptions.)

   _____ Are my facts correct?

   _____ Do my details really prove my point?

4. **Skills**

   _____ Have I spelled all words correctly?

   _____ Have I used correct grammar?

   _____ Have I corrected all errors in punctuation and capitalization?

   _____ Can my handwriting be read easily? Have I written in pen?

Organization

Topic Sentences 1

A *paragraph* is a group of sentences that express a central point. The *topic sentence* is the most important part of a paragraph because it shows the main idea in the paragraph. Writing clear topic sentences helps you state your ideas in a logical way or, in other words, the way that makes the most sense.

What Is a Topic Sentence?

The *topic sentence* of the paragraph states the main idea. The topic sentence is the sentence that tells what the paragraph is all about. It will be the broadest statement in the passage. The other sentences tell more about the topic sentence. Every *detail,* or small piece of information in the passage, gives information to support or explain the topic sentence. The following diagram illustrates this:

Topic Sentence

↓   ↓   ↓   ↓

Detail   Detail   Detail   Detail

Here is an example:

Topic Sentence: The United States won 13 medals at the 1994 Winter Olympics.

↓   ↓   ↓   ↓

Detail:	**Detail:**	**Detail:**	**Detail:**
Bonnie Blair won two gold medals in speed skating.	The U.S. won four medals in Alpine skiing.	Nancy Kerrigan won a silver medal in figure skating.	In the women's moguls, Liz McIntyre won a silver medal.

Quick Quiz A

Directions: Fill out the chart by writing the details that support the main idea of this paragraph.

The unit price is the price per unit of measure of an item. Items can be measured by weight, such as ounces, pounds, or grams. Items can be measured by volume, such as fluid ounces, cups, and quarts. Items can be measured by length, such as inches, feet, or yards. The unit price helps you compare different sizes and brands of the same item.

Topic Sentence: The unit price is the price per unit of measure of an item.

Detail	Detail	Detail
_____	_____	_____
_____	_____	_____
_____	_____	_____
_____	_____	_____

Where Do I Put the Topic Sentence in a Paragraph?

In most cases, the topic sentence will be the first sentence in a paragraph. Below are two examples. The topic sentence is underlined in each paragraph:

- Topic sentence at the *beginning* of a paragraph:

Passage 1

<u>Some cars cost more to insure than other cars</u>. As you shop for a new car, keep in mind the car's design and accident history. Cars with fancier designs such as Jaguars and Mercedes usually cost more to insure than economy cars. Cars that have a poor safety record such as the Chevy Corvair cost more to insure than cars with a good safety record.

Passage 2

<u>The Florida landscape has a great variety of plant life</u>. Some Florida woodlands are filled with majestic pine trees. Hardwood trees such as swamp maples, bald cypresses, bays, and oaks grow in some of the state's forests. Other wooded areas are a mix of different types and species of plant life. Dozens of different kinds of subtropical trees can be found in the Florida Keys.

However, you do not have to place the topic sentence first in a paragraph. You can place it in the middle or at the end of a paragraph as well. Here are some examples:

- Topic sentence in the *middle* of a paragraph:

Clothing can be made of natural materials. These come from plants or animals. Cotton, wool, silk, and linen are all natural materials. <u>Clothing labels tell you what materials are in your clothes.</u> Clothing can also be made of synthetic materials. These are made of chemicals. Rayon and polyester are synthetic materials.

- Topic sentence at the *end* of a paragraph:

The tape heads of VCRs need to be cleaned every few months. Lint should be removed from washing-machine filters. The coils at the back of refrigerators need to be vacuumed to remove dust. <u>Doing simple repairs to your appliances can make them last longer.</u>

Quick Quiz B

Directions: Underline the topic sentence in each paragraph.

1. Under federal law, when you shop by mail or phone, you receive certain protections not available if you shop in a store. For example, under the Mail Order Rule, companies are required to ship your order within the time period promised in their advertisement. If no time period is promised, the company must ship your order within 30 days after they receive it. In either case, when there is a delay, the company must send you an option notice. This option notice tells you of a shipping delay and gives you the choice of agreeing to the delay or canceling your order and receiving a prompt refund.

2. Most stores carry three different brands of the same items. First, there are name brands. These are advertised on television and radio. As a result, they are the most familiar items. Second, there are house brands. These products often carry the store's name on them. Sometimes, the store will put a special name on them instead of the store's name. Often, house brands are made by the same companies that make name brands. Last, stores carry generic or no-frills brands. These come in very simple packages. They are not advertised. They are the least expensive brands.

3. Buying by mail-order catalogs offers convenience. The item is sent right to your house. This is very convenient if you do not have a car and live far from the stores. You also save time by buying from catalogs. You do not have to spend hours looking for an item in a store. Mail order catalogs also offer a great variety of products. Some catalogs have more than 1,000 pages of items! Buying by mail-order catalogs offers many advantages.

4. The federal court system in America is like a pyramid. The state courts are on the bottom and federal courts are in the middle. At the very top of the pyramid is the Supreme Court, the "court of last resort." The nine Supreme Court Justices have the power to try cases that have not been previously tried by a lower court. Each year, the Supreme Court Justices receive more than 5,000 petitions to review such decisions. They accept only the most important of these.

5. Green turtles are captured for their meat and their eggs. These are eaten by people throughout the world. Hawkbill turtles are valued mainly for their shells. However, their meat and eggs are also eaten. Sea turtles provide many products for people. Loggerhead turtles are not often eaten since their meat has a strong flavor, but their large shells are used as decorations.

Answers to Quick Quizzes

Answers to Quick Quiz A

Topic Sentence: The unit price is the price per unit of measure of an item.

↓	↓	↓
Detail	**Detail**	**Detail**
Items can be measured by weight, such as ounces, pounds, or grams.	Items can be measured by volume, such as fluid ounces, cups, or quarts.	Items can be measured by length, such as inches, feet, or yards.

Answers to Quick Quiz B

1. Under federal law, when you shop by mail or phone, you receive certain protections not available if you shop in a store.

2. Most stores carry three different brands of the same items.

3. Buying by mail-order catalogs offers many advantages.

4. The federal court system in America is like a pyramid.

5. Sea turtles provide many products for people.

Practice Test

Directions: Choose the <u>one best answer</u> to each question.

Questions 1–2 refer to the following paragraph:

(1) "Full" warranties give full repairs or replacement for a period of time. (2) Sometimes, the warranty can cover the entire life of the product. (3) During this period, the product will be repaired or you will get a new one. (4) A "limited" warranty promises less. (5) That's because it limits the owner's rights. (6) The warranty is only good for a certain period of time. (7) The product will be covered for 30 days, 60 days, or 90 days, for example. (8) Not all the parts will be covered, either.

1. Which sentence would be most effective at the beginning of this paragraph?

   (1) Every product carries a warranty.

   (2) The heating elements may be covered, but not the knobs.

   (3) Always read your warranties.

   (4) Guarantees and warranties can be either "full" or "limited."

   (5) Be sure to save all warranties.

2. Which revision would improve the effectiveness of this document?

   Begin a new paragraph with

   (1) sentence 3.

   (2) sentence 4.

   (3) sentence 5.

   (4) sentence 6.

   (5) sentence 8.

Questions 3–4 refer to the following passage:

(1) Follow these directions to operate your vacuum cleaner. (2) To connect the power cord, pull the cord out. (3) A red band on the power cord indicates how far out you should pull it. (4) Do not pull the cord beyond that point. (5) Then connect the plug to the wall outlet. (6) The green control light should come on to indicate that power is available. (7) To start the cleaner, gently press the switch on the top of the unit. (8) To stop the machine, press the switch again. (9) Always turn the cleaner off before you disconnect the cord.

3. The topic sentence of this paragraph is

(1) sentence 1.

(2) sentence 2.

(3) sentence 3.

(4) sentence 4.

(5) sentence 5.

4. Which revision would make this document more effective?

Begin a new paragraph with

(1) sentence 5.

(2) sentence 6.

(3) sentence 7.

(4) sentence 8.

(5) sentence 9.

Question 5 refers to the following paragraph:

Credit can help you when you are short on cash. Credit can also be safer than cash. With credit, you do not have to carry a lot of cash that can be lost or stolen. Cash cannot be replaced if it is lost or stolen. Credit can be traced so you are protected against theft or loss. With credit, you can shop when items are on sale, too. This can help you save money.

5. Which sentence would be most effective at the *beginning* of this paragraph?

(1) Some forms of credit are easier to use than personal checks.

(2) With some forms of credit, you do not have to prove who you are.

(3) Credit is not free, however.

(4) Credit allows you to buy something now and pay for it in the future.

(5) There are several advantages to buying with credit.

Answers

1. **The correct answer is (4).** The sentence *Guarantees and warranties can be either "full" or "limited"* states the main idea of the paragraph: the two kinds of warranties. That is why it is the best choice for the topic sentence.

2. **The correct answer is (2).** The sentence *A "limited" warranty promises less* introduces the second main idea, so it would be the best choice as a topic sentence for a second paragraph.

3. **The correct answer is (1).** The sentence *Follow these directions to operate your vacuum cleaner* states the main idea of the paragraph. Thus, it is the best topic sentence.

4. **The correct answer is (3).** The first half of the paragraph concerns connecting the power cord. The second half concerns operating the vacuum cleaner. Thus, the best choice for a new topic sentence is *To start the cleaner, gently press the switch on the top of the unit.*

5. **The correct answer is (5).** The paragraph describes the positive aspects of credit, so the best choice for a topic sentence is *There are several advantages to buying with credit.*

Unity and Coherence 2

How can you make your writing well-organized and clear? In this lesson, you will learn how *unity* can help your writing stay on the subject. When your writing stays on the subject, it has *coherence*.

What Are Unity and Coherence?

When people cooperate with one another, they can achieve their goals more easily. In the same way, when all the sentences in a paragraph are on the same topic, the paragraph works as one unit and thus achieves its purpose. A paragraph has *unity* and *coherence* if all of its sentences support the same main idea. *Unity* and *coherence* are lost if the paragraph goes off the topic by including sentences that do not relate to the main idea.

The writer of the following paragraph achieved unity by linking every detail to the topic sentence:

(1) Lightning bolts have tremendous heat, power, and danger. (2) These streaks of electricity heat the air around them to 20,000 degrees Fahrenheit or even more. (3) A lightning bolt lasts a fraction of a second, but it has enough power—30 million volts—to light up most of New York City. (4) Because lightning bolts can be more powerful than an atomic bomb, they can cause severe injuries and even death.

(1) Topic sentence: lightning bolts
(2) Lightning bolts' heat
(3) Lightning bolts' power
(4) Lighting bolts' danger

Creating Paragraph Unity

To unify your paragraphs, you should

1. write a topic sentence that states one main idea,

2. link every sentence to the topic sentence,

3. put only one main idea in each paragraph,

4. start a new paragraph every time you begin a new idea, and

5. use transitions to link ideas.

Below is the first draft of a paper about another fierce kind of storm: tornadoes. It lacks unity because two sentences do not relate to the topic sentence. The two sentences have been crossed out. On the lines provided, explain why the sentences do not belong in the paragraph.

(1) A tornado is a dangerous storm because of its swiftly spinning winds and unpredictable path. (2) A tornado's winds can spin at more than 300 miles per hour! (3) ~~We have many hurricanes in my neighborhood~~. (4) When nearby, a tornado usually sounds like the roaring of hundreds of airplanes. (5) A tornado's whirling winds smash down on homes, stores, and cars, often causing much damage. (6) ~~There was a tornado in my neighborhood last year, but we were lucky to be at my grandmother's house at the time~~.

Sentence 3 does not belong because

_____

Sentence 6 does not belong because

_____

The paragraph's topic sentence explains that the paragraph is about the dangers of tornadoes. You can see that sentences 3 and 6 are off the topic. Sentence 3 discusses hurricanes, even though the paragraph describes tornadoes. Sentence 6 tells about the writer's experiences with tornadoes, but does not mention any danger.

Quick Quiz A

Directions: Below is the first draft of a paper. It lacks unity and coherence because three sentences are off the topic. Find the three sentences and cross them out. On the lines provided, explain why the sentences do not belong in the paragraph.

(1) Tidal waves are another type of frightening storm. (2) During a tidal wave, a wall of water 25 feet high can rush to shore, pushed by 200-mile-per-hour winds. (3) I am afraid of hurricanes but not tidal waves.

(4) Called "tsunamis," these fierce tidal waves are caused by earth-quakes in the middle of the ocean. (5) Weather satellites are a costly way to track storms. (6) Most tsunamis start along the "Ring of Fire." (7) This is a zone of volcanoes 24,000 miles long in the Pacific Ocean. (8) The Hawaiian Islands are pretty but I would not like to live there.

1. Sentence ___ does not belong because

_____

2. Sentence ___ does not belong because

_____

3. Sentence ___ does not belong because

_____

Quick Quiz B

Directions: Below is a topic sentence for a paragraph about storms. Complete the paragraph by selecting the five details that fit. Cross out the three details that do not support the topic sentence. Then write the paragraph on the lines provided. Use the details in the order in which they are given.

Details to Choose

1. Storms account for nearly all of the most costly disasters in America.

2. The costliest disaster in American history is Hurricane Andrew, the storm that ravaged Florida and Louisiana in 1992.

3. My dog hides under the bed when he hears thunder.

4. Hurricane Andrew left $15.5 billion in damage.

5. Storms are most common on the east coast during the fall.

6. Tornadoes also cause a lot of damage.

7. My friend Jean lives in the Midwest.

8. The Xenia tornadoes that occurred in 1974 in the Midwest left $1.3 billion in damage.

Topic sentence: Every year, storms kill and injure thousands of people around the world and cause billions of dollars worth of damage.

_____

_____

_____

_____

Use Transitions

As you read earlier, you can also use *transitions* to link ideas. Transitions are clue words that show how ideas are related. Choosing the correct transition helps you create unity and coherence by joining related ideas. The following chart shows some transitions and the links they create.

Relationship	Transition
addition	and, also, plus, in addition to, as well as, with, furthermore, moreover, besides, therefore
contrast	but, however, nevertheless, on the other hand, on the contrary, although, or, nor, yet
time, order	before, since, first, second, third (etc.), then, last, next, subsequently
example	for example, for instance, when
result	because, consequently, as a result, then, for, so, if

Quick Quiz C

Directions: Choose the correct transition to complete each sentence.

1. Turn the water off all the way (and, but) fix any leaks.

2. Even a small drip uses up a lot of water (if, as well as) costing you money!

3. Turn off the radio and TV (plus, when) you are not watching or listening to them.

4. Try not to open the refrigerator often (because, on the other hand) this makes the refrigerator work harder to cool the food.

5. (But, In addition) turn down the heat in the winter to save on fuel bills.

Answers to Quick Quizzes

Answers to Quick Quiz A

1. Sentence 3 is off the topic because it describes the writer's feelings about storms, which does not relate to the topic sentence.

2. Sentence 5 is off the topic because it describes tracking storms. This topic is not part of the paragraph.

3. Sentence 8 is off the topic. The sentence describes the writer's feelings about Hawaii, which is not related to tidal waves.

Answers to Quick Quiz B

Every year, storms kill and injure thousands of people around the world and cause billions of dollars worth of damage. Storms account for nearly all of the most costly disasters in America. The costliest disaster in American history is Hurricane Andrew, the storm that ravaged Florida and Louisiana in 1992. Hurricane Andrew left $15.5 billion in damage. Tornadoes also cause a lot of damage. The Xenia tornadoes that occurred in 1974 in the Midwest left $1.3 billion in damage.

Sentences 3, 5, and 7 were left out because they are off topic. They do not support the topic sentence.

Answers to Quick Quiz C

1. and
2. as well as
3. when
4. because
5. In addition

Practice Test

Directions: Choose the <u>one best answer</u> to each question.

Questions 1–5 refer to the following instructions.

Using Your Toaster

(1) Remove all labels from your toaster. (2) Then wipe the toaster down with a clean, wet cloth. (3) Close the tray before plugging the toaster into the wall outlet. (4) This will get rid of the odor of the new heating element. (5) Before toasting for the first time, preheat the toaster without inserting any bread. (6) To toast, push the toasting lever until it locks into position. (7) This will lower the food into the slot and switch on the heating element. (8) Toast tastes best with butter and jelly. (9) Do not place any object on top of the toaster for warming.

1. Which revision would make these instructions more effective?

   (1) Switch the order of sentences 1 and 2

   (2) Switch the order of sentences 2 and 3

   (3) Switch the order of sentences 4 and 5

   (4) Switch the order of sentences 6 and 7

   (5) Switch the order of sentences 8 and 9

2. What transition could be added to sentence 1?

   (1) For example

   (2) Then

   (3) First

   (4) Because

   (5) Nevertheless

3. Which sentence is off the topic?

   (1) Sentence 2

   (2) Sentence 5

   (3) Sentence 7

   (4) Sentence 8

   (5) Sentence 9

4. What transition could be added to sentence 9?

    (1) Since

    (2) Before

    (3) Next

    (4) For instance

    (5) Last

5. Which sentence best concludes these instructions?

    (1) Your toaster depends on the free flow of air to stay cool.

    (2) Betty bought a toaster oven at a local appliance store.

    (3) Everyone needs a toaster.

    (4) Toasters break down often but they are easy to repair.

    (5) In conclusion, toast is easy to make.

Answers

1. **The correct answer is (3).** The correct order of the sentences is *Before toasting for the first time, preheat the toaster without inserting any bread. This will get rid of the odor of the new heating element.*

2. **The correct answer is (3).** The writer could add the transition "first" to signal to the reader that this is the first step in the instructions.

3. **The correct answer is (4).** Sentence 8 has nothing to do with the passage because it is not part of the instructions.

4. **The correct answer is (5).** The writer can add the transition "last" to signal to the reader that this is the conclusion of the instructions.

5. **The correct answer is (1).** The sentence *Your toaster depends on the free flow of air to stay cool* directly follows from the previous sentence *Do not place any object on top of the toaster for warming.* This creates unity and coherence.

Sentence Structure

Sentence Fragments 3

The three most common sentence errors are *fragments, run-ons,* and *comma splices.* In this chapter, you will learn how to correct these sentence errors.

Fragments

A sentence is a group of words that expresses a complete idea. Every complete sentence has a *subject* (noun or pronoun), a *predicate* (verb or verb phrase), and expresses a complete thought.

A *fragment* is a group of words that does not express a complete thought. Fragments are created when

- a subject is missing,
- a verb is missing,
- both a subject and verb are missing, or
- the word group does not express a complete thought.

Examples of Fragments	
No subject:	**No verb:**
Have wings that do not help in flying.	The penguins in the South Pole.
No subject or verb:	**Not a complete thought:**
Thousands of miles every year.	If you visit the pyramids.

Don't be fooled by a capital letter at the beginning of a word group or a period at the end. Just because a group of words starts with a capital letter and ends with a period does not make it a sentence.

Quick Quiz A

Directions: Put a check next to those items that are fragments.

_____**1.** Getting a good job.

_____**2.** Is very unhealthy for people, plants, and animals.

_____**3.** Working for several years and studying for the GED at the same time.

_____**4.** A group of people who study together.

_____**5.** Some big companies in the area.

Correcting Fragments

You can correct a fragment by adding the missing parts. In the examples below, the added parts are underlined.

Correcting Fragments	
Fragment	Sentence
Have wings that do not help in flying.	<u>Penguins</u> have wings that do not help in flying.
The penguins in the South Pole.	The penguins in the South Pole <u>live in packs</u>.
Thousands of miles every year.	<u>The salesman travels</u> thousands of miles every year.
If you visit the pyramids.	If you visit the pyramids, <u>bring me a gift!</u>

Quick Quiz B

Directions: Correct each fragment by adding the missing parts in order to form complete sentences.

1. Have become polluted.

   _____

   _____

2. Is very unhealthy for people, plants, and animals.

   _____

   _____

3. Have dumped sewage into rivers, causing pollution.

   _____

   _____

4. Some big factories in the area.

   _____

   _____

5. Because people assumed rivers would carry away the waste.

   _____

   _____

Run-Ons and Comma Splices

A *run-on sentence* is two incorrectly joined independent clauses. Run-ons are created when two sentences are run together without any punctuation. When a comma is used instead of a semicolon (;), colon (:), or coordinating conjunction to join two complete sentences, the error is called a *comma splice*.

Examples of Run-on Sentences and Comma Splices

Run-ons

Day ended at dusk drivers pulled their wagons into a circle.

The people put up tents oxen grazed in the circle.

Comma Splices

Day ended at dusk, drivers pulled their wagons into a circle.

The people put up tents, oxen grazed in the circle.

Quick Quiz C

Directions: Put a check next to the run-ons.

_____**1.** The first pioneers moved West in the 1760s; the second group came 80 years later.

_____**2.** Daniel Boone connected trails he helped many pioneers.

_____**3.** The Wilderness Road was the best route through the mountains over 200,000 pioneers traveled on it.

_____**4.** Some pioneers traveled by the Ohio River it was an easier route than the mountains.

_____**5.** Later the pioneers took the boats apart they used the wood for their houses.

Correcting Run-Ons and Comma Splices

There are four ways to correct a run-on or comma splice:

Comma Splice: Daniel Boone connected trails, he helped many pioneers.

1. *Divide the words into two complete sentences.*

   Daniel Boone connected trails. He helped many pioneers.

2. *Add a conjunction* (and, nor, but, or, for, yet, so) *to create a compound sentence.*

   Daniel Boone connected trails, so he helped many pioneers.

3. *Add a subordinating conjunction to create a complex sentence.*

   Because Daniel Boone connected trails, he helped many pioneers.

4. *Use a semicolon to create a compound sentence.*

   Daniel Boone connected trails; he helped many pioneers.

Quick Quiz D

Directions: Correct each run-on or comma splice. Use one of the four methods described above.

1. The Wilderness Road was the best route through the mountains over 200,000 pioneers traveled on it.

   _____

   _____

2. Some pioneers traveled by the Ohio River it was an easier route than the mountains.

   _____

   _____

3. Later the pioneers took the boats apart they used the wood for their houses.

   _____

   _____

4. Settlers built log cabins they had to cut all the logs by hand.

   _____

   _____

5. Families ate cornbread they fed the leftovers to the hogs.

   _____

   _____

Answers to Quick Quizzes

Answers to Quick Quiz A

Every item is a fragment.

Possible Answers to Quick Quiz B

1. Many rivers have become polluted.
2. Pollution is very unhealthy for people, plants, and animals.
3. Factories have dumped sewage into rivers, causing pollution.
4. Some big factories in the area are cleaning up pollution.
5. Because people assumed rivers would carry away the waste, they did not worry about pollution.

Answers to Quick Quiz C

Only sentence 1 is correct. All other sentences are run-ons.

Possible Answers to Quick Quiz D

1. The Wilderness Road was the best route through the mountains, so over 200,000 pioneers traveled on it.
2. Some pioneers traveled by the Ohio River because it was an easier route than the mountains.
3. Later the pioneers took the boats apart, and they used the wood for their houses.
4. Settlers built log cabins. They had to cut all the logs by hand.
5. Families ate cornbread; they fed the leftovers to the hogs.

Practice Test

Directions: Choose the <u>one best answer</u> to each question.

Questions 1–5 refer to the following memo.

(1) All employees required to attend a meeting on April 1 to discuss the new health plan. (2) The meeting will be held in the Conference Room on the second floor the meeting will start promptly at 11:00. (3) Ms. Emma Sands of HealthSmart will explain your health-care options, she will answer any questions you have. (4) Bring your own lunch soda and coffee will be available. (5) This is a very important matter, be sure to attend.

1. Which correction should be made to sentence 1?

    (1) Add *are* before <u>required</u>

    (2) Change <u>required</u> to <u>requiring</u>

    (3) Add a comma after <u>April 1</u>

    (4) Add a period after <u>meeting</u>

    (5) Change <u>required</u> to <u>are requiring</u>

2. Which correction should be made to sentence 2?

    (1) Add a comma after <u>Room</u>

    (2) Change <u>will be held</u> to <u>holding</u>

    (3) Add a semicolon after <u>floor</u>

    (4) Add a comma after <u>floor</u>

    (5) Put a period after <u>meeting</u>

3. Which correction should be made to sentence 3?

    (1) Remove the comma

    (2) Change the comma to a semicolon

    (3) Change <u>will explain</u> to <u>explaining</u>

    (4) Take away <u>will explain</u>

    (5) Capitalize <u>she</u>

4. Which correction should be made to sentence 4?

   (1) Put a comma after <u>soda</u>

   (2) Put a comma after <u>and</u>

   (3) Change <u>bring</u> to <u>bringing</u>

   (4) Put a comma after <u>lunch</u>

   (5) Put a period after <u>lunch</u> and capitalize <u>soda</u>

5. Which correction should be made to sentence 5?

   (1) Remove the comma

   (2) Capitalize <u>be</u>

   (3) Put a comma after <u>very</u>

   (4) Put a period after <u>important</u>

   (5) Add *so* before <u>be sure to attend</u>

Answers

1. **The correct answer is (1).** As written, the sentence is missing part of the verb, so you have to add *are*.

2. **The correct answer is (3).** The run-on occurs between <u>floor</u> and <u>meeting</u>. Only choice (3) corrects this sentence error.

3. **The correct answer is (2).** This is a comma splice. Only choice (2) corrects the error by correctly joining the two sentences.

4. **The correct answer is (5).** The run-on occurs between <u>lunch</u> and <u>soda</u>. Only choice (5) corrects this error.

5. **The correct answer is (5).** This is a comma splice. You can join the two sentences with the coordinating conjunction *so*.

Coordination and Subordination 4

Too many short sentences create a boring style. They may also make it difficult for the reader to understand your ideas. If you combine the short sentences by using *coordination* and *subordination,* you can link your ideas and keep your reader interested.

What Is Coordination in Sentences?

Sentence *coordination* links ideas that are equally important. Follow these steps to achieve coordination:

- Decide which ideas can and should be combined. Choose ideas that go together.

- Coordinate the clauses or the sentences that show the appropriate relationship between ideas.

Coordinating with Coordinating Conjunctions

The seven coordinating conjunctions are *for, and, nor, but, or, yet, so.* When you coordinate two complete sentences with a coordinating conjunction, you create a *compound sentence.* Each of the coordinating conjunctions has a different meaning. Choose the coordinating conjunction that shows the right relationship between sentences.

Coordinating Conjunction	Meaning	Function
for	because	to show cause
and	also	to link ideas
nor	negative	to reinforce negative
but, yet	however	to contrast ideas
or	choice	to show possibilities
so	therefore	to show results

Study these examples:

Your refrigerator is frost-proof,   so   you won't have to defrost it.

Sentence #1   *Coordinating*   *Sentence #2*
                      conjunction

This sentence shows *result*: Because your refrigerator is frost-proof, you won't have to defrost it.

Look at this example:

I want to take the job,   but   the commute is too long.

Sentence #1   *Coordinating*   *Sentence #2*
                      conjunction

This sentence shows *contrast*: The speaker wants the job; however, the commute is too long.

Quick Quiz A

Directions: Choose the conjunction that best coordinates each pair of sentences.

1. I bought a new outfit for the interview, (so, and) I made sure that I got a good night's sleep before the interview.

2. Randi is going to ask her mother to drive her to the interview, (or, but) she will take the bus that leaves from her corner.

3. Sal knows that he interviews well, (or, but) he is always interested in improving his skills.

4. Chivon already has a good part-time job, (nor, yet) she is looking for a job that offers more challenges.

5. Natalie always does her best, (for, or) she knows that hard work helps her get ahead.

Coordinate Carefully

Be careful not to connect unrelated ideas or connect too many ideas in one sentence. These problems with coordinating sentences confuse your readers and make it hard to understand your ideas. Here are some examples:

Unrelated ideas linked:	Lucas has to photocopy the papers, but he is wearing a blue shirt to work today. (The second part of the sentence has nothing to do with the first part.)
Related ideas linked:	Lucas has to photocopy the papers, but the photocopy machine is broken today.
Too many ideas linked:	Melvin bought a CD player, but it did not work very well, so he decided to return the CD player to the store, but he could not remember where he had put the receipt, so he was annoyed at himself.
Improved:	Melvin bought a CD player, but it did not work very well. As a result, he decided to return the CD player to the store. However, he could not remember where he had put the receipt, so he was annoyed at himself.

What Is Subordination in Sentences?

When you subordinate one part of a sentence, you make the dependent, or subordinate, clause develop the independent, or main, clause. Subordination helps you show specific relationships between ideas. It also helps you to emphasize one idea over the other.

- *Coordinate* sentence parts when you want to link related independent clauses.

- *Subordinate* sentence parts when you want to put the most important idea in the main clause and give less importance to the idea in the dependent clause.

Follow these four steps to subordinate sentence ideas:

1. Decide which idea or clause is the most important.

2. Make this idea the "main clause."

3. Choose the subordinating conjunction that best expresses the relationship between the main clause and the dependent clause.

4. Join the clauses correctly.

There are many subordinating conjunctions, including:

as	after	although	because	before
if	once	since	so	though
than	that	unless	until	unless
when	wherever	whether	where	while

Below are some examples of effective sentence subordination. Notice the different ways to subordinate ideas. The subordinating conjunction is underlined.

Not Subordinated: You buy a product. You should save the receipt.

Subordinated: <u>When</u> you buy a product, you should save the receipt.

OR

You should save the receipt <u>when</u> you buy a product.

Not Subordinated: You repair the machine. You may get a raise.

Subordinated: <u>If</u> you repair the machine, you may get a raise.

OR

You may get a raise <u>if</u> you repair the machine.

Quick Quiz B

Directions: Combine each pair of sentences to create subordination.

1. You apply for a job. Be sure to find out as much as you can about the company.

_____

_____

2. It is well worth your effort. It may be difficult to get this information.

_____

_____

3. Talk to people who work at the company. Do you know anyone there?

_____

_____

4. Read stock reports about the company. Find out if they are a profitable company.

_____

_____

5. You need to get the facts. You will have a hard time being persuasive without them.

_____

_____

Answers to Quick Quizzes

Answers to Quick Quiz A

1. and

2. or

3. but

4. yet

5. for

Possible Answers to Quick Quiz B

1. Before you apply for any job, be sure to find out as much as you can about the company.

2. Although it may be difficult to get this information, it is well worth your effort.

3. Talk to people who work at the company, if you know anyone there.

4. Read stock reports about the company so you know if they are a profitable company.

5. Unless you get the facts, you will have a hard time being persuasive.

PracticeTest

Directions: Choose the <u>one best answer</u> to each question.

Questions 1–5 refer to the following paragraph.

(1) In some states, you must have a certain amount of insurance. (2) This is true even if you do not plan to drive your car on public highways! (3) In New York State, you must have a minimum amount of liability coverage. (4). Other people can be protected in case you cause an accident. (5) Collision and comprehensive coverage cost the most. (6) You can reduce these costs by buying a policy with high deductibles. (7) Young men pay more than other drivers. (8) Young men cause more accidents. (9) Your insurance will cost more. (10) Did you get several traffic tickets or have you been in an accident?

1. Which is the most effective combination of sentences 1 and 2?

   (1) In some states, you must have a certain amount of insurance, if you do not plan to drive your car on public highways!

   (2) If you do not plan to drive your car on public highways, you must in some states have a certain amount of insurance.

   (3) In some states, you must have a certain amount of insurance, even if you do not plan to drive your car on public highways!

   (4) In some states, you must have a certain amount of insurance do not plan to drive your car on public highways!

   (5) In some states, you must have a certain amount of insurance, so this is true even if you do not plan to drive your car on public highways!

2. Which is the most effective combination of sentences 3 and 4?

   (1) In New York State, you must have a minimum amount of liability coverage, and other people can be protected in case you cause an accident.

   (2) In New York State, you must have a minimum amount of liability coverage other people can be protected in case you cause an accident.

   (3) In New York State, you must have a minimum amount of liability coverage, other people can be protected in case you cause an accident.

   (4) In New York State, you must have a minimum amount of liability coverage, so other people can be protected in case you cause an accident.

   (5) People can be protected in case you cause an accident in New York State, yet you must have a minimum amount of liability coverage.

3. Which is the most effective combination of sentences 5 and 6?

(1) Collision and comprehensive coverage cost the most you can reduce these costs by buying a policy with high deductibles.

(2) You can reduce these costs by buying a policy with high deductibles, yet collision and comprehensive coverage cost the most.

(3) Collision and comprehensive coverage cost the most, since you can reduce these costs by buying a policy with high deductibles.

(4) Collision and comprehensive coverage cost the most, but you can reduce these costs by buying a policy with high deductibles.

(5) You can reduce these costs by buying a policy with high deductibles unless collision and comprehensive coverage cost the most.

4. Which is the most effective combination of sentences 7 and 8?

(1) Young men pay more than other drivers because they cause more accidents.

(2) Young men cause more accidents because they pay more than other drivers.

(3) Young men cause more accidents unless they pay more than other drivers.

(4) Young men pay more than other drivers so they cause more accidents.

(5) Young men pay more than other drivers, yet they cause more accidents.

5. Which is the most effective combination of sentences 9 and 10?

(1) Your insurance will cost more unless you have gotten several traffic tickets or have been in an accident.

(2) You have gotten several traffic tickets or have been in an accident since your insurance will cost more.

(3) You have gotten several traffic tickets or have been in an accident but your insurance will cost more.

(4) Although you have gotten several traffic tickets or have been in an accident, your insurance will cost more.

(5) Your insurance will cost more if you have gotten several traffic tickets or have been in an accident.

Answers

1. **The correct answer is (3).**
2. **The correct answer is (4).**
3. **The correct answer is (4).**
4. **The correct answer is (1).**
5. **The correct answer is (5).**

Dangling and Misplaced Modifiers | 5

Modifiers are words that describe. There are two kinds of modifiers: adjectives and adverbs. Errors occur when adjectives and adverbs are used incorrectly. Two of the most common errors are *dangling modifiers* and *misplaced modifiers*.

What Are Dangling Modifiers?

What is wrong with the following sentence?

> *Walking down the stairs, the clock struck ten.*

As it's written, the sentence states that the clock was walking down the stairs. We know that clocks can't walk. The error occurs because the phrase "walking down the stairs" has nothing to modify or describe. Remember that a *modifier* is a word or phrase that gives more information about the subject, verb, or object in a clause. A *dangling modifier* is a word or phrase that describes something that has been left out of the sentence.

Correcting Dangling Modifiers

Since the basic problem with a dangling modifier is that it relates to a word that is not actually in the sentence, you must come up with a noun or pronoun that the dangling modifier can be linked to. In other words, you must make the *connection* between the modifier and the word or phrase it modifies. There are different ways that you can rewrite a sentence that has a dangling modifier, as long as it makes sense. Here are two examples:

Dangling: *Giving a party, several balloons were blown up.*

Correct: *When they gave a party, they blew up several balloons.*

                 (Now, <u>they</u> are the ones blowing up the balloons.)

Dangling: *Do not ride the bike without being fully assembled.*

Correct: *You should not ride the bike unless it is fully assembled.*

                 (Now, <u>you</u> are the one who should not ride the bike unless it is assembled.)

Quick Quiz A

Directions: Explain the dangling modifier in each sentence.

1. Stored under the bed for 20 years, the owner of the stamps decided to sell them.

_____

_____

2. Important facts might be revealed when leaving.

_____

_____

3. While driving into town, a crash was seen.

_____

_____

4. While eating lunch, a bug slipped into her soup.

_____

_____

5. Sailing up the river, the New York skyline was seen.

_____

_____

Quick Quiz B

Directions: Rewrite each of the following sentences to correct the dangling modifier.

1. Stored under the bed for 20 years, the owner of the stamps decided to sell them.

   _____

   _____

2. Important facts might be revealed when leaving.

   _____

   _____

3. While driving into town, a crash was seen.

   _____

   _____

4. While eating lunch, a bug slipped into her soup.

   _____

   _____

5. Sailing up the river, the New York skyline was seen.

   _____

   _____

What Are Misplaced Modifiers?

What is wrong with the following sentence?

We bought a kitten for my sister we call Fluffy.

As this sentence is written, it means that the sister, not the kitten, is named Fluffy. That's because the modifier "we call Fluffy" is in the wrong place in the sentence. This error is called a *misplaced modifier*. A *misplaced modifier* is a phrase, clause, or word placed too far from the word or words it modifies (describes).

Correcting Misplaced Modifiers

To correct a misplaced modifier, move the modifier as close as possible to the word or phrase it describes. Here is how the previous incorrect sentence should read:

We bought a kitten we call Fluffy for my sister.

Below are two more examples:

Misplaced: *The student was referred to a tutor with learning disabilities.*

Correct: *The student with learning disabilities was referred to a tutor. (Now, the student, rather than the tutor, has the learning disabilities.)*

Misplaced: *Danielle found a sweater in the car that doesn't belong to her.*

Correct: *Danielle found a sweater that doesn't belong to her in the car. (Now, the sweater, not the car, doesn't belong to Danielle.)*

Quick Quiz C

Directions: Explain the misplaced modifier in each sentence.

1. The golfer made a hole-in-one with the green shirt.

_____

_____

2. The house was rebuilt by the people destroyed by the fire.

_____

_____

3. We saw many beautiful homes driving through the South.

_____

_____

4. Jen bought a ring from a jeweler with diamonds.

_____

_____

5. We need someone to take care of a dog who does not smoke or drink.

_____

_____

Quick Quiz D

Directions: Rewrite each of the following sentences to correct the misplaced modifier.

1. The golfer made a hole-in-one with the green shirt.

_____

_____

2. The house was rebuilt by the people destroyed by the fire.

_____

_____

3. We saw many beautiful homes driving through the South.

_____

_____

4. Jen bought a ring from a jeweler with diamonds.

_____

_____

5. We need someone to take care of a dog who does not smoke or drink.

_____

_____

Answers to Quick Quizzes

Answers to Quick Quiz A

1. This sentence states that the owner of the stamps was stored under the bed for 20 years.

2. According to this sentence, the facts are leaving.

3. This sentence states that the crash is doing the driving.

4. According to this sentence, the bug is eating lunch.

5. This sentence states that the New York skyline is sailing up the river.

Possible Answers to Quick Quiz B

1. The owner decided to sell the stamps, which had been stored under the bed for 20 years.

2. You might reveal important facts when you leave.

    -or-

    Important facts might be revealed when you leave.

3. While we were driving into town, we saw a crash.

    -or-

    While driving into town, we saw a crash.

4. While Kris was eating lunch, a bug slipped into her soup.

5. As we sailed up the river, we saw the New York skyline.

Answers to Quick Quiz C

1. This sentence states that the hole-in-one, not the golfer, is wearing a green shirt.

2. According to this sentence, the people, not the house, were destroyed in the fire.

3. This sentence states that the homes, not the people, were driving through the South.

4. According to this sentence, the jeweler (not the ring) had diamonds.

5. This sentence states that the dog does not drink or smoke.

Possible Answers to Quick Quiz D

1. The golfer with the green shirt made a hole-in-one.

2. The house destroyed by the fire was rebuilt by the people.

3. Driving through the South, we saw many beautiful homes.

4. Jen bought a ring with diamonds from a jeweler.

5. We need someone who does not smoke or drink to take care of a dog.

Practice Test

Directions: Choose the <u>one best answer</u> to each question.

Questions 1–5 refer to the following field report.

(1) The huge construction site commanded our attention entering the field. (2) The lumber was reported delivered by the watchman that was dried. (3) The contractor climbed the scaffolding wearing a hardhat. (4) While pouring the concrete, a tree fell into the foundation. (5) The company almost made a profit of $150,000 on this job.

1. Which correction should be made to sentence 1?

   (1) Change <u>entering the field</u> to <u>enter the field</u>

   (2) Change <u>entering the field</u> to <u>having entered the field</u>

   (3) Insert a comma after <u>our attention</u>

   (4) Change <u>entering the field</u> to <u>by entering the field</u>

   (5) Change <u>entering the field</u> to <u>as we entered the field</u>

2. Which revision would best improve sentence 2?

   (1) The watchman that was dried reported that the lumber was delivered.

   (2) The lumber that was dried was reported delivered by the watchman.

   (3) The watchman, that was dried, reported that the lumber was delivered.

   (4) The lumber reported that it was dried and delivered.

   (5) The lumber was reported delivered by the dried watchman.

3. Which revision would best improve sentence 3?

   (1) The contractor climbed the scaffolding which was wearing a hardhat.

   (2) The contractor wearing a hardhat climbed the scaffolding.

   (3) The scaffolding wearing a hardhat was climbed by the contractor.

   (4) The contractor climbing the scaffolding wearing a hardhat.

   (5) A hardhat worn by the contractor climbed the scaffolding.

4. Which correction should be made to sentence 4?

    (1) Change <u>a tree fell</u> to <u>a tree was falling</u>

    (2) Add a semicolon after <u>concrete</u>

    (3) Delete the comma after <u>concrete</u>

    (4) Change <u>While pouring</u> to <u>While the masons were pouring</u>

    (5) Change <u>While pouring</u> to <u>While poured</u>

5. Which correction should be made to sentence 5?

    (1) Add a comma after <u>profit</u>

    (2) Add a semicolon after <u>profit</u>

    (3) Change <u>almost made a profit</u> to <u>made a profit of almost</u>

    (4) Change <u>almost</u> to <u>about</u>

    (5) Replace <u>almost</u> with <u>nearly</u>

Answers

1. **The correct answer is (5)**. Only choice (5) corrects the dangling participle by providing the subject.

2. **The correct answer is (2).** As the sentence reads, the watchman—not the lumber—was dried. Choice (2) best corrects the misplaced modifier.

3. **The correct answer is (2).** As the sentence reads, the scaffolding—not the contractor—was wearing a hardhat. Choice (4) is not a complete sentence. Choice (2) best corrects the misplaced modifier.

4. **The correct answer is (4).** Only choice (4) corrects the dangling participle by providing the subject the participle modifies.

5. **The correct answer is (3).** The misplaced modifier *almost* implies that no profit was made. However, the writer intended to state that the company made a large profit of almost $150,000.

Parallel Structure 6

Parallel structure means putting ideas in the same grammatical structure: matching words, phrases, and clauses. Parallel structure helps make your writing sound smooth and logical.

Parallel Words

Parallel words share the same part of speech. They can be nouns, adjectives, or verbs, for example. To build a parallel structure, they must all be the same part of speech in a sentence. If they are verbs, the words must also be in the same tense. This means they must all be in the past, present, or future. Two or more words can be parallel. Below are some examples. The words are underlined and labeled.

Parallel Nouns:	We ate <u>pizza</u>, <u>soda</u>, and <u>salad</u>.
	noun noun noun
Parallel Adjectives:	The students were <u>kind</u> and <u>smart</u>.
	adj. adj.
Parallel Verbs:	Let's <u>swim</u>, <u>skate</u>, and <u>jog</u>.
(present tense)	*verb verb verb*
Parallel Verbs:	Javier <u>studied</u>, <u>ate</u>, and <u>rested</u>.
(past tense)	*verb verb verb*

Since parallelism has to do with the sound of language, try to read your sentences aloud as you write. This will help you hear whether the sentence parts are parallel.

Quick Quiz A

Directions: Choose the word or phrase that completes the parallel structure in each sentence.

1. The photographer knew about composition and (lighting, how to control the lights).

2. Television is good for the news, movies, and (to watch sports, sports).

3. You should eat foods that are nourishing and (taste good, tasty).

4. Lin doesn't know if she should study or (sleep, sleeping).

5. Cotton is comfortable and (you can wash it, washable).

6. John seemed tired and (disappointed, a disappointed person).

7. The child was spoiled and (annoying, annoyed me).

8. Last-minute studying is not as effective as (to keep, keeping up) with the work.

9. Today, airplanes are fast and (flying safely, safe).

10. Our neighbor is helpful, friendly, and (talks a lot, talkative).

Parallel Phrases

A *phrase* is a group of words that does not have a subject or a verb. Here are some examples:

to work hard	to study long hours	eating hot dogs
keeping up with the neighbors	over the rainbow	into the woods

Parallel phrases create effective, clear writing. In these phrases, two or more parts are parallel. Below are some examples. The phrases are underlined and labeled.

I expected the child <u>to be angry</u> and <u>to pout.</u>
             "to" phrase   *"to" phrase*

<u>Passing the GED</u>, <u>earning a high school diploma</u>, and <u>getting a good job</u>
"-ing" phrase   *"-ing" phrase*   *"-ing" phrase*
are Rita's goals.

Rich, <u>the captain of the football team</u> and <u>the president of the senior class,</u>
        noun phrase   *noun phrase*
has a big ego.

Quick Quiz B

Directions: Choose the phrase that completes the parallel structure in each sentence.

1. To do a good job, you have (to plan, planning) beforehand.
2. The job has great hours and (a fair salary, paying a good salary).
3. Polyester clothing washes easily, dries quickly, and (never wrinkles, coming out without wrinkles).
4. Shoshana's ambition is to be a doctor and (specializing, to specialize) in surgery.
5. To avoid getting hit by lightning, never seek protection under a tree, lie down on wet ground, or (stay on a bike, staying on a bike).
6. The kids chased each other across the lawns, down the streets, and (they ran into the store, into the store).
7. Tom realized that it was time for him to grow up and (facing, to face) reality.
8. Tom was willing to change, but he was immature and (had no confidence, wanting to be more confident).
9. Tom had three things in his favor: a good work ethic, a willingness to learn, and (a determination to succeed, determined to succeed).
10. Tom started with a trip to the local community college, and then (took out a loan, taking out a loan) from a credit union.

Parallel Clauses

A *clause* is a group of words that has a subject and a verb. A clause that expresses a complete idea is called an *independent clause*. It is also called a *sentence*. Here are some examples:

- I completed a computer training class at Hudson Institute.
- I have a great deal of training in computers.

A clause that does *not* express a complete thought is called a *dependent clause*. It is also called a *fragment*. Here are some examples:

- Having completed a computer training class at Hudson Institute. (missing a subject)
- Because I have a great deal of training in computers. (not a complete thought)

Parallel clauses create effective, clear writing. In these clauses, two or more clauses will be parallel. Below are some examples. The clauses are underlined and labeled.

<u>Our classes are full</u>, <u>our instructors are all hired</u>, and
independent clause   *independent clause*

<u>we anticipate a great semester.</u>
    independent clause

<u>Since all classes are filled</u>, <u>no additional students will be accepted.</u>
    dependent clause   *independent clause*

Be sure to include in the second part of the sentence all the words you need to make the sentence clear. For example:

Not parallel: *Ricardo was torn between his love for his job and his family.*

Parallel: *Ricardo was torn between his love for his job and his <u>love for his</u> family.*

Quick Quiz C

Directions: Circle the word, phrase, or clause that completes the parallel structure. Write a sentence explaining your reasoning.

1. The great white shark located its prey, circled it slowly, and (attacks it quickly, attacked it quickly).

   _____

   _____

2. My sister likes ice cream and (eating salty pretzels, salty pretzels).

   _____

   _____

3. He wore clothes that were better (than, than those of) the other students.

   _____

   _____

4. My teacher has a harsh voice, a stern manner, and (is very stocky in build, a stocky build).

   _____

   _____

5. Compare your grades for this semester (with last quarter, with your grades from last quarter).

   _____

   _____

Answers to Quick Quizzes

Answers to Quick Quiz A

1. lighting

2. sports

3. tasty

4. sleep

5. washable

6. disappointed

7. annoying

8. keeping up

9. safe

10. talkative

Answers to Quick Quiz B

1. to plan

2. a fair salary

3. never wrinkles

4. to specialize

5. stay on a bike

6. into the store

7. to face

8. had no confidence

9. a determination to succeed

10. took out a loan

Answers to Quick Quiz C

1. attacked it quickly

To make the phrases parallel, you need to match the verb tenses: *located* and *circled* are both in the past tense, so *attacked* must be in the past tense as well.

2. salty pretzels

Ice cream and *salty pretzels* are parallel.

3. than those of

The phrase *than those of* is necessary to make the parallelism complete. Otherwise, the sentence does not make sense.

4. a stocky build

A stocky build makes the parallelism of the phrases *a harsh voice* and *a stern manner* complete.

5. with your grades from last quarter

The phrase *with your grades from last quarter* is necessary to make the parallelism complete. Otherwise, the sentence does not make sense.

Practice Test

Directions: Choose the <u>one best answer</u> to each question.

Questions 1–5 refer to the following paragraph.

(1) The Human Resources department approved the first request for medical leave time, but not the second person asking. (2) To succeed, you will need patience, determination, and to have support. (3) If you are asking for leave time, be sure to have a doctor's note stating your condition and writing a memo explaining how much time you need. (4) Depending on your condition, this will be an easy procedure or a procedure that is a difficult one. (5) The process is long but necessary.

1. Sentence 1: **The Human Resources department approved the first request for medical leave, but not <u>the second person asking</u>.**

   Which is the best way to write the underlined portion of this sentence?

   (1) No change

   (2) asked the second one

   (3) the second one

   (4) asking the second one

   (5) to ask the second one

2. Sentence 2: **To succeed, you will need patience, determination, and <u>to have support</u>.**

   Which is the best way to write the underlined portion of this sentence?

   (1) No change

   (2) support

   (3) having support

   (4) being supported

   (5) support is also important

3. Sentence 3: **If you are asking for leave time, be sure to have a doctor's note stating your condition and <u>writing a memo explaining how much time you need</u>.**

   Which is the best way to write the underlined portion of this sentence?

   (1) No change

   (2) to write a memo explaining how much time you need

   (3) having written a memo explaining how much time you need

   (4) a memo explaining how much time you will need

   (5) having written a memo explaining how much time you need

4. Sentence 4: **Depending on your condition, this will be an easy procedure or <u>a procedure that is a difficult one</u>.**

Which is the best way to write the underlined portion of this sentence?

(1) No change

(2) to be a difficult one

(3) being a difficult one

(4) a procedure one

(5) a difficult one

5. Sentence 5: **The process is long but <u>necessary</u>.**

Which is the best way to write the underlined portion of this sentence?

(1) No change

(2) being necessary

(3) insisting on being necessary

(4) having been necessary

(5) you can find it necessary

Answers

1. **The correct answer is (3).** The phrases *first request for medical leave time* and *the second one* must be parallel.

2. **The correct answer is (2).** The nouns *patience, determination,* and *support* must be parallel.

3. **The correct answer is (4).** The phrases *a doctor's note stating your condition* and *a memo explaining how much time you will need* must be parallel.

4. **The correct answer is (5).** The phrases *easy procedure* and *difficult one* must be parallel. Each phrase has an adjective and a noun.

5. **The correct answer is (1).** The adjectives *long* and *necessary* must be parallel.

Usage

Subject-Verb Agreement 7

Agreement means matching subject and verb in a sentence. When subjects and verbs agree, your sentences sound smooth and correct.

Singular and Plural

Singular subjects agree with singular verbs. Plural subjects agree with plural verbs.

- *Singular* means one.
- *Plural* means more than one.

In English, only nouns and pronouns can be singular and plural. Study these examples:

Singular (One)	Plural (More Than One)
I	we
he, she, it	them
baby	babies
dog	dogs

Quick Quiz A

Directions: Circle the <u>singular</u> word in each line.

1. raccoons	rocket	readers
2. nose	colors	gorillas
3. chair	animals	problems
4. machines	cookies	carpet
5. cape	students	hills

Directions: Circle the <u>plural</u> word in each line.

6. star	planet	pictures
7. key	kitten	pancakes
8. telephone	flowers	bracelet
9. pencils	it	paper
10. shoe	rings	he

Singular Subjects

If the subject is singular, add *-s* or *-es* to your verb. For example:

A <u>diamond</u>   <u>sparkle</u>s.   One <u>rabbit</u>   <u>hop</u>s.

singular subject   singular verb   singular subject   singular verb

Plural Subjects

If the subject is plural, use the base form of the verb. Do not add any ending to the verb. Here are some base forms of verbs:

sparkle	run	eat	sleep	skip
hop	study	work	swim	ski

Below are some examples of plural subjects that agree with their verbs:

The <u>diamonds</u>   <u>sparkle</u>.   The <u>rabbits</u>   <u>hop</u>.

Plural subject   plural verb   plural subject   plural verb

Quick Quiz B

Directions: Complete each sentence with the correct verb. Circle the verb.

1. The crop (grow, grows) fast in the summer.
2. The crops (grow, grows) slowly in the fall.
3. She (walks, walk) to the park.
4. They (walks, walk) to the park.
5. A kitten (climbs, climb) the new chair.
6. Several kittens (climbs, climb) the new chair.
7. One apple (falls, fall) off the big tree.
8. Many apples (falls, fall) off the big tree.
9. A firefighter (battle, battles) the huge blaze.
10. Many firefighters (battle, battles) the huge blaze.

Quick Quiz C

Directions: Fill in each blank with the correct form of the verb in the parentheses ( ). Here is an example:

1. One boy   _____ (say)
   Two boys   _____
   Answer: One boy <u>says</u>
             Two boys <u>say</u>

You may have to change the spelling of the verb to get the correct form.

2. A surfer   _____ (like)
   Many surfers   _____

3. An airplane   _____ (fly)
   Four airplanes   _____

4. She   _____ (travel)
   We   _____

5. One burger   _____ (cook)
   Many burgers   _____

6. A knife   _____ (slice)
   Many knives   _____

7. He   _____ (sleep)
   They   _____

8. One student   _____ (read)
   Several students   _____

9. A pencil   _____ (break)
   Many pencils   _____

10. A doctor   _____ (operate)
    Many doctors   _____

The Verbs *To Be* and *To Have*

These verbs do not follow a pattern because they are irregular. Here are some examples:

Present Tense of *To Be*:

The <u>car</u>	<u>is</u> fast.	The <u>cars</u>	<u>are</u> fast.
singular subject	*singular verb*	*plural subject*	*plural verb*

Past Tense of *To Be*:

The <u>car</u>	<u>was</u> fast.	The <u>cars</u>	<u>were</u> fast.
singular subject	*singular verb*	*plural subject*	*plural verb*

Present Tense of *To Have:*

The <u>dog</u>	<u>has</u> fleas.	The <u>dogs</u>	<u>have</u> fleas.
singular subject	*singular verb*	*plural subject*	*plural verb*

Past Tense of *To Have*:

The <u>dog</u>	<u>had</u> fleas.	The <u>dogs</u>	<u>had</u> fleas.
singular subject	*singular verb*	*plural subject*	*plural verb*

Remember how to change the verbs *to be* and *to have* to show singular and plural.

To Be		To Have	
Present	Past	Present	Past
I <u>am</u>	I <u>was</u>	I <u>have</u>	I <u>had</u>
you <u>are</u>	you <u>were</u>	you <u>have</u>	you <u>had</u>
he/she/it <u>is</u>	he/she/it <u>was</u>	he/she/it <u>has</u>	he/she/it <u>had</u>
we <u>are</u>	we <u>were</u>	we <u>have</u>	we <u>had</u>
they <u>are</u>	they <u>were</u>	they <u>have</u>	they <u>had</u>
who <u>is</u>	who <u>was</u>	who <u>has</u>	who <u>had</u>

Quick Quiz D

Directions: Fill in each blank with the correct form of the verb in the parenthesis ( ). The first one is done for you. You will have to change the spelling of the verb.

1. present tense: This sandwich _____ a good snack.   (to be)

   Answer: This sandwich <u>is</u> a good snack.

2. present tense: The sandwiches _____ a good snack. (to be)

3. past tense: This sandwich _____ a good snack.   (to be)

4. past tense: The sandwiches _____ a good snack. (to be)

5. present tense: The dog _____ a bone.   (to have)

6. present tense: The dogs _____ many bones.   (to have)

7. past tense: The dog _____ a bone.   (to have)

8. past tense: The dogs _____ many bones.   (to have)

I and *You*

I is singular. *You* can be both singular or plural. Nonetheless, *I* and *you* are always used with the base form of the verb. Here are some examples:

- I talk (not *I talks*)   you talk (not *you talks*)
- I hope (not *I hopes*)   you hope (not *you hopes*)
- I want (not *I wants*)   you want (not *you wants*)

And and *Or*

Two singular subjects joined by *and* form a plural subject. Here are some examples:

> <u>An apple and an orange</u> <u>are</u> good for you.
> *two singular subjects joined by* and, *plural verb*

> <u>Luke and Michelle</u> <u>were</u> at my party.
> *singular subjects joined by* and, *plural verb*

Two singular subjects joined by *or* form a singular subject. Here are some examples:

> <u>An apple or an orange</u> <u>is</u> a great snack.
> *singular subjects joined by* or, *singular verb*

> <u>Luke or Michelle</u> <u>cheers</u> for my team.
> *singular subjects joined by* or, *singular verb*

Quick Quiz E

Directions: Complete each sentence with the correct verb. Circle the verb.

1. I (sleep, sleeps) late on weekends.
2. You (jog, jogs) in the park, even in the rain!
3. I (study, studies) late into the night.
4. You (race, races) sports cars at the track.
5. The toaster and the oven (is, are) broken.
6. The toaster or the oven (is, are) broken.
7. Melinda and Jessica (attend, attends) dancing school.
8. Melinda or Jessica (attend, attends) dancing school.
9. The cookie and the cake (has, have) too many calories.
10. The cookie or the cake (has, have) been eaten!

Answers to Quick Quizzes

Answers to Quick Quiz A

1. rocket
2. nose
3. chair
4. carpet
5. cape
6. pictures
7. pancakes
8. flowers
9. pencils
10. rings

Answers to Quick Quiz B

1. grows
2. grow
3. walks
4. walk
5. climbs
6. climb
7. falls
8. fall
9. battles
10. battle

Answers to Quick Quiz C

1. says, say
2. likes, like
3. flies, fly
4. travels, travel
5. cooks, cook
6. slices, slice
7. sleeps, sleep
8. reads, read
9. breaks, break
10. operates, operate

Answers to Quick Quiz D

1. is

2. are

3. was

4. were

5. has

6. have

7. had

8. had

Answers to Quick Quiz E

1. sleep

2. jog

3. study

4. race

5. are

6. is

7. attend

8. attends

9. have

10. has

Practice Test

Directions: Choose the <u>one best answer</u> to each question.

Questions 1–5 refer to the following memo.

(1) The window have jammed so please do not try to open it. (2) You needs to call maintenance to get it repaired. (3) The heating system and the lighting system is equally delicate, so please do not attempt to adjust them. (4) While we appreciates your help, repairing the heating and cooling systems are not part of your job. (5) Workers has better ways to spend their time while they are in the office.

1. Which correction should be made to sentence 1?

   (1) Change <u>try</u> to <u>tries</u>

   (2) Change <u>try</u> to <u>tried</u>

   (3) Change <u>try</u> to <u>be trying</u>

   (4) Change <u>have</u> to <u>has</u>

   (5) Change <u>have</u> to <u>were</u>

2. Which correction should be made to sentence 2?

   (1) Change <u>needs</u> to <u>needing</u>

   (2) Change <u>needs</u> to <u>need</u>

   (3) Change <u>needs</u> to <u>are needing</u>

   (4) Change <u>get</u> to <u>gets</u>

   (5) Change <u>gets</u> to <u>getting</u>

3. Which correction should be made to sentence 3?

   (1) Change <u>adjust</u> to <u>adjusts</u>

   (2) Change <u>attempt</u> to <u>attempts</u>

   (3) Change <u>adjust</u> to <u>adjusts</u>

   (4) Change <u>is</u> to <u>were</u>

   (5) Change <u>is</u> to <u>are</u>

4. Which correction should be made to sentence 4?

   (1) Change <u>appreciates</u> to <u>appreciate</u>

   (2) Change <u>help</u> to <u>helps</u>

   (3) Change <u>are</u> to <u>was</u>

   (4) Change <u>help</u> to <u>helps</u>

   (5) Change <u>are</u> to <u>is</u>

5. Which correction should be made to sentence 5?

    (1) Change <u>ways</u> to <u>way</u>

    (2) Change <u>spend</u> to <u>spends</u>

    (3) Change <u>are</u> to <u>was</u>

    (4) Change <u>has</u> to <u>have</u>

    (5) Change <u>are</u> to <u>is</u>

Answers

1. **The correct answer is (4).** The singular subject *window* takes the singular verb *has*.

2. **The correct answer is (2).** *You* is always used with the base form of the verb. Here, the base form is *need*.

3. **The correct answer is (5).** Two singular subjects joined by *and* form a plural subject. The two subjects are *heating system* and *lighting system*. Use the plural verb *are*.

4. **The correct answer is (1).** If the subject is plural, use the base form of the verb. Do not add any ending to the verb. The plural subject *we* takes the plural verb *appreciate*.

5. **The correct answer is (4).** If the subject is plural, use the base form of the verb. Do not add any ending to the verb. The plural subject *workers* takes the plural verb *have*.

Verb Tense | 8

Verbs change form to show time. In grammar, time is called *tense*.

Regular Verbs

Some verbs are *regular*. This means they form the past tense and past participle by adding *-d* or *-ed* to the present form. The vowel does not change. Here are some examples:

Present Tense	Past Tense	Past Participle	
Add *-d*	I bake	I baked	I have baked
Add *-d*	I change	I changed	I have changed
Add *-ed*	I learn	I learned	I have learned
Add *-ed*	I earn	I earned	I have earned

Irregular Verbs

Irregular verbs don't form the past by adding *-ed* or *-d*. The past tense and past participle are formed in many different ways.

- Sometimes, a vowel changes and *-n* or *-en* is added. For example,

Present Tense	Past Tense	Past Participle
begin	began	begun
drive	drove	driven
eat	ate	eaten
fall	fell	fallen
forgive	forgave	forgiven
give	gave	given

- Other times, the verbs change their vowel and add -*t*. For example,

Present Tense	Past Tense	Past Participle
bend	bent	bent
catch	caught	caught
kneel	knelt	knelt
lose	lost	lost

- Or, they may not change at all. For example,

Present Tense	Past Tense	Past Participle
burst	burst	burst
hurt	hurt	hurt
put	put	put
set	set	set

Spelling Changes

There are two spelling changes that affect verbs.

1. When a verb ends in -*y*, you usually change the -*y* to -*i* before you add -*ed* to form the past tense. For example,

Present Tense	Past Tense
try	tried
cry	cried
identify	identified
justify	justified

2. When you have a base verb that ends with a consonant preceded by a short vowel, you usually double the consonant before adding -*ed* to the past tense. For example,

Present Tense	Past Tense
drip	dripped
chip	chipped
skip	skipped
spot	spotted

Quick Quiz A

Directions: Choose the correct form of each misspelled verb. You may wish to use a dictionary to check the spelling of some verbs.

1. I (gave, gived) the paper to my boss.

2. The cut was not deep, but it (hurted, hurt) a lot nonetheless.

3. The rain (began, begined) just when the batter hit the first ball.

4. The driveway was (froze, frozen) solid.

5. Mother (hid, hided) the household chemicals in a safe place.

6. We could tell her leg was (broke, broken).

7. Johnny (caught, catched) the fly ball.

8. We (loosed, lost) our way on the deserted back road.

9. The boy (shaked, shook) with cold.

10. Which dessert have you (chosed, chosen)?

Quick Quiz B

Directions: Complete the chart with the correct form of each verb. You may wish to use a dictionary to check the spelling of some verbs.

Present Tense	Past Tense	Past Participle
1. catch	_____	_____
2. do	_____	_____
3. drink	_____	_____
4. fly	_____	_____
5. get	_____	_____ or _____
6. go	_____	_____
7. hold	_____	_____
8. know	_____	_____
9. sink	_____	_____
10. take	_____	_____
11. teach	_____	_____
12. wear	_____	_____

Lie and *Lay*

Lie means "to rest." *Lay* means "to put down." *Lie* is an irregular verb. *Lay* is a regular verb. Because *lay* is both the present tense of *lay* and the past tense of *lie*, many people use *lay* when they mean *lie*. Study this chart to further clarify *lie* and *lay*.

Verb	*Meaning*	*Examples*
lay	to put down	present tense: The cat lies down.
		past tense: The cat lay down.
		future tense: The cat will lie down.
		perfect tense: The cat has lain down.
lie	to rest	present tense: Lay your paper down.
		past tense: He laid the paper down.
		future tense: He will lay the paper down.
		perfect tense: She has laid the paper down.

Use the Same Tense for all Words in a Sentence or Passage

What is wrong with the following sentence?

I am walking down the hall, and I saw my friend.

The writer started out in the present tense (*am walking*) and changed to the past tense (*saw*). You should always *choose one tense and stay with it in the entire essay*. Do not switch tenses in the middle of a sentence or an essay.

Here are two ways to correct this sentence:

Present tense: *I <u>am walking</u> down the hall, and I <u>see</u> my friend.*

Past tense: *I <u>was walking</u> down the hall, and I <u>saw</u> my friend.*

Quick Quiz C

Directions: Complete each sentence by choosing the correct verb.

1. We had many customers yesterday, and the store (was, is) very busy.

2. Today, it is not as crowded but many people (are, were) crowded around the sale racks.

3. Last week, I jogged around the block and (saw, see) other runners.

4. The snow started early but we (knew, know) it would not stick on the ground.

5. I took my sister to the park, where she (fell, falls) off the swing.

Active and Passive Voice

Verbs also show *voice*, the form of the verb that shows whether the subject performs the action or received the action. English verbs have two voices: *active* and *passive*.

1. A verb is *active* when the subject performs the action, as in these examples:

   - You made a mistake.
   - We bought a muffin.

2. A verb is *passive* when its action is performed upon the subject, as in these examples:

   - A mistake was made by you. (Or: A mistake was made.)
   - A muffin was bought by us.

In general, use the active voice instead of the passive voice. The active voice is less wordy and more direct than the passive voice.

Quick Quiz D

Directions: Rewrite each passive sentences into the active voice.

1. The GED Test was passed by Christine.

_____

_____

2. The dog was walked by Mark.

_____

_____

3. Checking in must be done by 9:00 every morning by you.

_____

_____

Answers to Quick Quizzes

Answers to Quick Quiz A

1. gave

2. hurt

3. began

4. frozen

5. hid

6. broken

7. caught

8. lost

9. shook

10. chosen

Answers to Quick Quiz B

	Present Tense	Past Tense	Past Participle
1.	catch	caught	caught
2.	do	did	done
3.	drink	drank	drunk
4.	fly	flew	flown
5.	get	got	gotten or got
6.	go	went	gone
7.	hold	held	held
8.	know	knew	known
9.	sink	sank	sunk
10.	take	took	taken
11.	teach	taught	taught
12.	wear	wore	worn

Answers to Quick Quiz C

1. was

2. are

3. saw

4. knew

5. fell

Answers to Quick Quiz D

1. Christine passed the GED Test.

2. Mark walked the dog.

3. You must check in by 9:00 every morning.

Practice Test

Directions: Choose the <u>one best answer</u> to each question.

Questions 1–5 refer to the following memo.

(1) Each employee has been gived a new identification card. (2) You should began using the card on April 30. (3) We have did this to make the office safer. (4) Wearing their cards must be done by employees at all times. (5) We known you will cooperate with this new rule. Thank you.

1. Which correction should be made to sentence 1?

   (1) Change <u>gived</u> to <u>giving</u>

   (2) Change <u>has been gived</u> to <u>has been give</u>

   (3) Change <u>has been gived</u> to <u>was gived</u>

   (4) Change <u>gived</u> to <u>given</u>

   (5) Change <u>gived</u> to <u>give</u>

2. Which correction should be made to sentence 2?

   (1) Change <u>began</u> to <u>begun</u>

   (2) Change <u>began</u> to <u>begin</u>

   (3) Change <u>began</u> to <u>beginning</u>

   (4) Change <u>began</u> to <u>begined</u>

   (5) Change <u>began</u> to <u>be beginning</u>

3. Which correction should be made to sentence 3?

   (1) Change <u>have did this</u> to <u>has done this</u>

   (2) Change <u>have did this</u> to <u>having done this</u>

   (3) Change <u>did</u> to <u>doing</u>

   (4) Change <u>did</u> to <u>do</u>

   (5) Change <u>did</u> to <u>done</u>

4. What is the best way to rewrite sentence 4?

   (1) Employees must wear their cards at all times.

   (2) At all times, wearing their cards must be done by employees.

   (3) By employees at all times wearing their cards must be done.

   (4) By employees wearing their cards must be done at all times.

   (5) To wear their cards must be done by employees at all times.

5. Which correction should be made to sentence 5?

   (1) Change <u>known</u> to <u>knewed</u>

   (2) Change <u>known</u> to <u>are knowing</u>

   (3) Change <u>known</u> to <u>is knowing</u>

   (4) Change <u>known</u> to <u>know</u>

   (5) Change <u>cooperate</u> to <u>cooperating</u>

Answers

1. **The correct answer is (4).** The sentence requires the past participle. The past participle of *give* is *given*.

2. **The correct answer is (2).** The sentence requires the present tense. The present tense of *begin* is *begin*.

3. **The correct answer is (5).** The sentence requires the past participle. The past participle of *do* is *done*.

4. **The correct answer is (1).** In general, use the active voice instead of the passive voice. The active voice is less wordy and more direct than the passive voice. Only the sentence in choice (1) is in the active voice.

5. **The correct answer is (4).** The sentence requires the present tense, *know*.

Mechanics

Capitalization 9

Capitalized Words

Capitalization tells readers when a new sentence is starting. Capitalization also points out specific words within a sentence.

Capitalize the First Word in a Sentence

Rule: Capitalize the first word in a sentence. This rule also covers dialogue, that is, a speaker's exact words. Here are some examples:

- Knowing how to write letters is important.
- "Are you taking the GED this year?" she asked.

Quick Quiz A

Directions: Circle the correct word to complete each sentence.

1. (according, According) to the latest census, Dade County is the largest county in Florida.
2. (The, the) Everglades became a national park in 1934.
3. "(Did, did) you ever visit Virginia Beach?" the travel agent asked.
4. (My, my) sister lives in Minnesota.
5. (many, Many) people visit California every year.

Capitalize Proper Nouns and Proper Adjectives

Rule: Capitalize proper nouns and proper adjectives. Here are some examples:

Proper nouns:	*Italy*	*Haiti*
Proper adjectives:	*Italian*	*Haitian*

Rule: Capitalize a person's name. Here are some examples:

Whitney Houston   *Yao Ming*   *Roberto Clemente*

Rule: Capitalize the title before a person's name. Here are some examples:

Ms.   *Mr.*   *Reverend*   *Dr.*   *Professor*

Rule: Capitalize abbreviations after a person's name. Here are some examples:

Martin Luther King, Jr.   *Beth Jobs, M.D.*

Rule: Capitalize the names of organizations, institutions, courses, and famous buildings. Here are some examples:

Organizations:	*Boy Scouts USA*	*The Girl Scouts of America*
Institutions:	*The United Nations*	*Major League Baseball*
Courses:	*French 101*	*Mathematics 203*
		(but not mathematics)
Buildings:	*Taj Mahal*	*Empire State Building*

Rule: Capitalize days, months, and holidays. Here are some examples:

Days:	*Monday*	*Tuesday*	*Wednesday*
Months:	*February*	*March*	*April*
Holidays:	*Thanksgiving*	*Fourth of July*	*Valentine's Day*

Quick Quiz B

Directions: Choose the correct word(s) in each line.

1. Iranian   iranian
2. halle berry   Halle Berry
3. dr. pepper   Dr. Pepper
4. Queen Latifa   queen latifa
5. Herman Goldish, M.D.   herman Goldish, m.d.
6. ms. Nolan   Ms. Nolan

Directions: Add capital letters as needed. The number in parentheses ( ) indicates the number of capital letters needed.

7. thank you for your inquiry about the wellbuilt company. (3)

8. we have offices in montana, ohio, and new jersey. (5)

9. candidates who speak spanish or italian are especially welcome. (3)

10. our offices are located in rockefeller center, new york. (5)

11. contact mr. joe brown or ms. tina faletta for more information. (7)

Directions: Choose the correct word in each line.

12. Thursday   thursday

13. mother's day   Mother's Day

14. Saturday   saturday

Rule: Capitalize geographical places and sections of the country. Here are some examples:

| Geographical places: | *Europe* | *Asia* | *Argentina* |

| Sections of the country: | *the South* | *the Midwest* | *the North* |

Rule: Capitalize the names of specific historical events, eras, and documents. Do not capitalize small words like *a, an,* and *the,* unless they are part of the title. Here are some examples:

| Historical events: | *Declaration of Independence* | *Great Depression* |

| Historical eras: | *Dark Ages* | *Renaissance* |

| Historical documents: | *Constitution* | *Bill of Rights* |

Quick Quiz C

Directions: Capitalize each of the following words and phrases correctly. Write your answers on the line.

1. revolutionary war   _____

2. magna carta   _____

3. korean war   _____

4. civil war   _____

5. jazz age   _____

6. harlem renaissance   _____

Rule: Capitalize the names of languages, nationalities, countries, and races. Here are some examples:

Languages:	*English*	*French*	*Creole*
Nationalities:	*American*	*Israeli*	*South African*
Countries:	*Ghana*	*Chile*	*China*
Races:	*Asian*	*Native-American*	*African-American*

Rule: Capitalize religions and references to the Supreme Being, including the pronouns referring to the Supreme Being. Here are some examples:

Judaism   Catholicism   Muslim   the Creator   Him   Heaven

Quick Quiz D

Directions: Capitalize each of the following words and phrases correctly. Write your answers on the line.

1. spanish   _____

2. german   _____

3. czech republic   _____

4. african   _____

5. christian scientist   _____

Capitalize Parts of Letters

Rule: Capitalize the greeting in a letter. Here are some examples:

> *Dear Ms. O'Connor:*   *Dear Aunt Ethel,*

Rule: Capitalize the first letter of the first word in the closing of a letter. Do not capitalize the other words. Here are some examples:

> *Sincerely yours,   Yours very truly,*

Quick Quiz E

Directions: Choose the correct word in each line.

1. Dear Dr. Carvo: dear dr. Carvo:

2. dear Hester,   Dear Hester,

3. Yours Truly,   Yours truly,

4. Best wishes,   Best Wishes,

Capitalize Titles

Rule: Capitalize the titles of books, plays, newspapers, and magazines. Do not capitalize the small words like *a, an,* and *the,* unless they begin the title. Here are some examples:

Book titles:	*Like Water for Chocolate*	*For Whom the Bell Tolls*
Play titles:	*The Agony and the Ecstasy*	*Hairspray*
Newspaper titles:	*The Cleveland Plain Dealer*	*The Los Angeles Times*
Magazine titles:	*Seventeen*	*Road and Track*

Answers to Quick Quizzes

Answers to Quick Quiz A

1. According
2. The
3. Did
4. My
5. Many

Answers to Quick Quiz B

1. Iranian
2. Halle Berry
3. Dr. Pepper
4. Queen Latifa
5. Herman Goldish, M.D.
6. Ms. Nolan
7. Thank you for your inquiry about the Wellbuilt Company.
8. We have offices in Montana, Ohio, and New Jersey.
9. Candidates who speak Spanish or Italian are especially welcome.
10. Our offices are located in Rockefeller Center, New York.
11. Contact Mr. Joe Brown or Ms. Tina Faletta for more information.
12. Thursday
13. Mother's Day
14. Saturday

Answers to Quick Quiz C

1. Revolutionary War
2. Magna Carta
3. Korean War
4. Civil War
5. Jazz Age
6. Harlem Renaissance

Answers to Quick Quiz D

1. Spanish
2. German
3. Czech Republic
4. African
5. Christian Scientist

Answers to Quick Quiz E

1. Dear Dr. Carvo:
2. Dear Hester,
3. Yours truly,
4. Best wishes,

Practice Test

Directions: Choose the <u>one best answer</u> to each question.

Questions 1–5 refer to the following letter.

(1) dear ms. reyes:

(2) I would like to apply for the job of truck driver advertised in sunday's *times*. (3) I am fluent in spanish and speak a little german. (4) I drove across america before settling in overland park, kansas, so I know our highways well. (5) I am available for an interview on mondays, thursdays, and fridays.

1. Which correction should be made to sentence 1?

   (1) Change <u>dear</u> to <u>Dear</u>

   (2) Change <u>ms.</u> to <u>Ms.</u>

   (3) Change <u>reyes</u> to <u>Reyes</u>

   (4) Change <u>dear</u> to <u>Dear</u>, <u>ms.</u> to <u>Ms.</u>, and <u>reyes</u> to <u>Reyes</u>

   (5) Change <u>ms.</u> to <u>Ms.</u> and <u>reyes</u> to <u>Reyes</u>

2. Which correction should be made to sentence 2?

   (1) Change <u>sunday's</u> to <u>Sunday's</u>

   (2) Change *<u>times</u>* to *<u>Times</u>*

   (3) Change *<u>times</u>* to *<u>TIMES</u>*

   (4) Change <u>truck driver</u> to <u>Truck Driver</u>

   (5) Change <u>sunday's</u> to <u>Sunday's</u> and *<u>times</u>* to *<u>Times</u>*

3. Which correction should be made to sentence 3?

   (1) Change <u>spanish</u> to <u>Spanish</u>

   (2) Change <u>spanish</u> to <u>Spanish</u> and <u>german</u> to <u>German</u>

   (3) Change <u>german</u> to <u>German</u>

   (4) Change <u>spanish</u> to <u>SPANISH</u>

   (5) Change <u>german</u> to <u>GERMAN</u>

4. Which correction should be made to sentence 4?

(1) Change <u>america</u> to <u>America</u>

(2) Change <u>america</u> to <u>America</u>, <u>overland park</u> to <u>Overland Park</u>, and <u>kansas</u> to <u>Kansas</u>

(3) Change <u>overland park</u> to <u>Overland Park</u>

(4) Change <u>kansas</u> to <u>Kansas</u>

(5) Change <u>highways</u> to <u>Highways</u>

5. Which correction should be made to sentence 5?

(1) Change <u>mondays</u> to <u>Mondays</u>

(2) Change <u>thursdays</u> to <u>Thursdays</u>

(3) Change <u>mondays</u> to <u>Mondays</u>, <u>thursdays</u> to <u>Thursdays</u>, and <u>fridays</u> to <u>Fridays</u>

(4) Change <u>fridays</u> to <u>Fridays</u>

(5) Change <u>mondays</u> to <u>Mondays</u> and <u>thursdays</u> to <u>Thursdays</u>

Answers

1. **The correct answer is (4).** Capitalize the greeting in a letter, the title before a person's name, and a person's name.

2. **The correct answer is (5).** Capitalize days of the week and the titles of newspapers.

3. **The correct answer is (2).** Capitalize the names of languages.

4. **The correct answer is (2).** Capitalize geographical places and sections of the country.

5. **The correct answer is (3).** Capitalize days of the week.

Punctuation | 10

Using the correct punctuation helps your readers understand your ideas more clearly. Here are the rules for using punctuation correctly.

The Comma

A comma, unlike a period, is merely used as a brief pausing point between two words. Commas are most commonly used to indicate that you should take a breath. As you read, take a look at where commas are used.

Use Commas with Dates and Numbers

Rule: Use a comma between the day of the month and the year. Here are some examples:

> *December 25, 2003*   *March 16, 1989*

Rule: Use commas to show thousands, millions, and so on. Put a comma after every three numbers. Here are some examples:

> *1,500*   *10,088*   *1,345,901*

Use Commas with Addresses

Rule: Use a comma to separate the parts of an address. Put commas between the street, town, and state. Don't put a comma between the state and the ZIP code. Here is an example:

> *We are visiting <u>671 Plitt Avenue</u>, <u>King City</u>, <u>California</u> <u>19393</u>*
>   *street*   *town*   *state* *ZIP code*

Use Commas in Letters

Rule: Use a comma after the greeting of an informal letter. Here are some examples:

> *Dear Kathy,*   *Dear Victoria,*

Rule: Use a comma at the close of any letter. Here are some examples:

> *Yours truly,*   *Sincerely,*

Use a Comma Between Parts of a Compound Sentence

A *compound sentence* has two or more independent clauses (simple sentences). The independent clauses can be joined with a coordinating conjunction (*and, but, or, nor, for, so,* and *yet.*) Use the comma *before* the coordinating conjunction that separates the two independent clauses. The coordinating conjunction and comma are underlined in the following examples.

> *You need a mortgage to buy a home, <u>so</u> be sure to apply for one.*
> sentence 1   sentence 2

> *Credit is often readily available, <u>but</u> it can be difficult to repay loans.*
> sentence 1   sentence 2

Quick Quiz A

Directions: Add commas as needed to the following letter.

(1) March 15 2001

(2) Ms. M. Susan Wilson
Frontier Magazine
650 S. Orcas St. Suite 103
Seattle WA 98108

Dear Ms. Wilson:

I would like to apply for the sales job advertised in my local newspaper. (3) I earned my GED last week and I am currently enrolled in Westside Community College.

1. Which correction should be made to reference 1?

   (1) Add a comma after <u>March</u>

   (2) Add a comma after <u>2001</u>

   (3) Add a comma after <u>15</u>

   (4) Add a comma after the <u>2</u> in 2001

   (5) Add a comma after <u>March</u> and after <u>15</u>

2. Which correction should be made to reference 2?

   (1) Add a comma after <u>St.</u>

   (2) Add a comma after <u>Magazine</u> and after <u>103</u>

   (3) Add a comma after <u>Seattle</u>

   (4) Add a comma after <u>Wilson</u> and after <u>Magazine</u>

   (5) Add a comma after <u>St.</u> and after <u>Seattle</u>

3. Which correction should be made to reference 3?

   (1) Add a comma after <u>GED</u>

   (2) Add a comma after <u>I</u>

   (3) Add a comma after <u>and</u>

   (4) Add a comma after <u>week</u>

   (5) Add a comma after <u>week</u> and after <u>and</u>

Use a Comma to Set Off a Direct Quotation

A *direct quotation* is a speaker's exact words. A direct quotation starts and ends with quotation marks. Here are some examples:

Speaker at the beginning:	*Cindi said, "It is warm enough to walk to work."*
Speaker at the end:	*"It is warm enough to walk to work," Cindi said.*
Speaker in the middle:	*"It is warm enough," Cindi said, "to walk to work."*

Use a Comma with Items in a Series

Rule: Use a comma between the items in a list. Here are some examples; notice the comma before the last item in the list.

We looked at sofas, chairs, and desks.

Letters must have your address, the date, the name of the person you are writing to, the body of the letter, a close, and your name.

Quick Quiz B

Directions: Add commas as needed.

1. You can get money orders at the bank credit union and post office.
2. A money order for $50 may cost 75 cents a money order for $100 may cost $1.00 and a money order for $500 may cost $2.00.
3. Banks sell money orders open checking accounts and issue credit cards.
4. To make a deposit, fill in your name address and account number on a deposit slip.
5. Check registers have spaces for you to record the check number date amount person or company and balance.

Use a Comma After Introductory Words

Rule: Use a comma after an opening phrase or clause. Below are some examples. In each sentence, the introductory part is underlined.

> *<u>When you open a checking account,</u> you will be given a check register.*

> *<u>In addition,</u> all banks issue a monthly statement.*

Quick Quiz C

Directions: Add a comma after each opening phrase or clause.

1. Like a money order a checking account solves the problem of carrying or mailing cash.

2. When you open a checking account at a bank you put some money into the account.

3. Instead of carrying cash you can carry a book of checks and write checks as you buy things.

4. If a check is lost or stolen call your bank and ask them to stop payment.

5. If someone tries to cash the check the bank will not pay out your money.

6. When you write a check you tell the bank to pay someone a specific amount of money.

The Semicolon

A semicolon looks like a period on top of a comma (;). A semicolon is stronger than a comma but not as strong as a period.

Rule: Use a semicolon between main clauses when the coordinating conjunction has been left out. Here are some examples:

Jana is a good friend; she is always there for me.
Antoine misplaced his wallet; he found it the next day.

Rule: Use a semicolon between main clauses connected by conjunctive adverbs such as *however, nevertheless, thus, moreover, for example,* and *consequently*. Here are some examples:

The parking lot is crowded; nevertheless, we got a good spot.
The trip to the Grand Canyon is expensive; however, we really want to visit this park.

Quick Quiz D

Directions: Add commas and semicolons as needed.

1. Real estate brokers can help you find an apartment however they charge fees for their services.

2. Sometimes the owner pays the fee other times the renter or buyer pays.

3. Always ask about the fees up front this way you won't be surprised by the cost.

4. A broker knows which homes are available consequently you can save a lot of time.

5. A broker will drive you to visit the apartments as a result you will not need a car.

The Colon

A colon looks like one period stacked on top of another one (:). The colon and semicolon may look a little alike, but they are very different marks of punctuation.

Rule: Use a colon after the opening of a business letter. Here are some examples.

Dear Ms. Robinson: *To Whom It May Concern:*

Rule: Use a colon before a list. Often, the word *following* will be used to introduce a list. Here is an example:

We need the following supplies: glue, tape, and paper.

Answers to Quick Quizzes

Answers to Quick Quiz A

1. **The correct answer is (3).**

2. **The correct answer is (5).**

3. **The correct answer is (4).**

Answers to Quick Quiz B

1. You can get money orders at the bank, credit union, and post office.

2. A money order for $50 may cost 75 cents, a money order for $100 may cost $1.00, and a money order for $500 may cost $2.00.

3. Banks sell money orders, open checking accounts, and issue credit cards.

4. To make a deposit, fill in your name, address, and account number on a deposit slip.

5. Check registers have spaces for you to record the check number, date, amount, person or company, and balance.

Answers to Quick Quiz C

1. Like a money order, a checking account solves the problem of carrying or mailing cash.

2. When you open a checking account at a bank, you put some money into the account.

3. Instead of carrying cash, you can carry a book of checks and write checks as you buy things.

4. If a check is lost or stolen, call your bank and ask them to stop payment.

5. If someone tries to cash the check, the bank will not pay out your money.

6. When you write a check, you tell the bank to pay someone a certain amount of money.

Answers to Quick Quiz D

1. Real estate brokers can help you find an apartment; however, they charge fees for their services.

2. Sometimes the owner pays the fee; other times the renter or buyer pays.

3. Always ask about the fees up front; this way you won't be surprised by the cost.

4. A broker knows which homes are available; consequently, you can save a lot of time.

5. A broker will drive you to visit the apartments; as a result, you will not need a car.

Practice Test

Directions: Choose the <u>one best answer</u> to each question.

Questions 1–5 refer to the following letter.

(1) Dear R. J. Mello

(2) On August 1 1994 I bought an Acme toaster oven (model 450T) from the Sav-More Appliance Store in St. Petersburg. I paid $29.99 for it. Enclosed is my receipt and the toaster oven.

(3) About a month after I purchased the toaster oven it overheated and burned everything I cooked in it. (4) On October 15, I took the toaster oven back to Sav-More Appliance I spoke with the manager, Ms. Kitter. (5) She told me, that the store could not replace the toaster after 30 days.

(6) I would like my money back so I can buy a different brand of toaster oven.

1. What correction should be made to sentence 1?

   (1) Add a comma after <u>Mello</u>

   (2) Add a semicolon after <u>Mello</u>

   (3) Add a comma after <u>R. J.</u> and after <u>Mello</u>

   (4) Add a semicolon after <u>R. J.</u>

   (5) Add a colon after <u>Mello</u>

2. What correction should be made to sentence 2?

   (1) Add a comma after <u>August 1</u> and after <u>1994</u>

   (2) Add a comma after <u>August 1</u>

   (3) Add a comma after <u>1994</u>

   (4) Add a semicolon after <u>Appliance Store</u>

   (5) Add a colon after <u>(model 450T)</u>

3. What correction should be made to sentence 3?

   (1) Add a colon after <u>oven</u>

   (2) Add a semicolon after <u>oven</u>

   (3) Add a comma after <u>oven</u>

   (4) Add a comma after <u>overheated</u>

   (5) Add a comma after <u>purchased</u>

4. What correction should be made to sentence 4?

    (1) Add a colon after <u>Appliance</u>

    (2) Add a comma after <u>Appliance</u>

    (3) Remove the comma after <u>October 15</u>

    (4) Add a comma after <u>back</u>

    (5) Add a semicolon after <u>Appliance</u>

5. What correction should be made to sentence 5?

    (1) Add a semicolon after <u>me</u>

    (2) Add a colon after <u>me</u>

    (3) Remove the comma after <u>me</u> and add a comma after <u>store</u>

    (4) Remove the comma after <u>me</u>

    (5) Remove the comma after <u>me</u> and add a colon after <u>store</u>

Answers

1. **The correct answer is (5).** Use a colon after the greeting of a business letter.

2. **The correct answer is (2).** Use a comma between the day of the month and the year; use a comma after an opening phrase.

3. **The correct answer is (3).** Use a comma after an opening phrase.

4. **The correct answer is (5).** Use a semicolon between main clauses when the coordinating conjunction has been left out.

5. **The correct answer is (4).** The sentence doesn't require the use of any commas.

Contractions and Possessive Pronouns | 11

It's important to use the exact word you want when you write. Otherwise, your writing will not convey your meaning. Contractions and possessive pronouns are often misused. A number of other English word pairs are also tricky to use correctly.

Using Contractions Correctly

A *contraction* is a shortened form of two words. To form a contraction, combine two words. Insert an apostrophe in the space where the letter or letters have been omitted.

Two Words	Letter or Letters Omitted	Contraction
I am	a	I'm
have not	o	haven't
can not	no	can't

The following chart shows how to spell the most common contractions.

Word + Word = Contraction	Word + Word = Contraction
does + not = doesn't	can + not = can't
could + not = couldn't	has + not= hasn't
he + is = he's	he + will = he'll
I + am = I'm	I + have = I've
it + is = it's	it + will = it'll
let + us = let's	must + not = mustn't
she + would = she'd	she + will = she'll
there + is = there's	they + are = they're
they + will = they'll	was + not = wasn't
we + are = we're	we + have = we've
we + would = we'd	we + will = we'll
were + not = weren't	who + is = who's
will + not = won't	would + not = wouldn't
you + are = you're	you + have = you've

Quick Quiz A

Directions: Make each of the following phrases into a contraction.

1. would not   _____

2. you are   _____

3. she would   _____

4. I will   _____

5. we will   _____

6. he is   _____

7. there is   _____

8. they are   _____

9. you are   _____

10. it is   _____

Contractions and Possessive Pronouns

Don't confuse *contractions* with *possessive pronouns*. Study the following chart to compare the two different parts of speech:

Contraction	Example	Possessive Pronoun	Example
it's (it is)	<u>It's</u> cold.	its	The dog wagged <u>its</u> tail.
you're (you are)	<u>You're</u> here!	your	Eat <u>your</u> dinner.
they're (they are)	<u>They're</u> nice.	their	The boys lost <u>their</u> mittens.
who's (who is)	<u>Who's</u> home?	whose	<u>Whose</u> hat is this?

Forming Possessive Pronouns

Possession shows ownership. Below are two ways to show possession:

The book that belongs to Hector.   *Hector's book*

While both ways of showing possession are correct, we usually use the second way—"Hector's book"—because it is less wordy.

In many languages other than English, the object possessed is named first, followed by the person or thing that possesses it. For example: *This is the office of Spencer.* As a result, the way possessives are formed in English often poses problems for non-native speakers. If English is not your first language, pay special attention to this next section. Follow these rules to spell possessive nouns correctly.

Rule: With singular nouns, add an apostrophe and an s to the word doing the owning.

Not possessive	Possessive
lion	lion's roar
Charles	Charles's job

Note: Often, people drop the *s* after the apostrophe in a singular possessive noun that ends in *s*. This is perfectly acceptable. So, instead of "Charle**s's** job," you can also write "Charle**s'** job."

Rule: With plural nouns ending is *s*, add an apostrophe after the *s* on the word doing the owning.

Not possessive	Possessive
clients	clients' receipts
workers	workers' ideas

Rule: With plural nouns not ending in *s*, add an apostrophe and an *s* on the word doing the owning.

Not possessive	Possessive
fish	fish's tails
women	women's trucks

Rule: To form the possessive of a business name, joint owner, or compound noun, put an apostrophe and *s* after the *last* word on the word doing the owning.

Not possessive	Possessive
Gilbert and Sullivan	Gilbert and Sullivan's operas
sister-in-law	sister-in-law's bracelet

Quick Quiz B

Directions: Underline the correct possessive form for each phrase. The first one is done for you.

1. the idea of Bill   <u>Bill's idea</u>   Bills' idea

2. the pets of Martha   Marthas pet's   Martha's pets

3. the pencil of Charles   Charles' pencil   Charle's pencil

4. the workers of the company company's workers'   company's workers

5. the job of Leslie   Leslie's job   Leslies' job

6. the shoes of Michel   Michel shoe's   Michel's shoes

7. the tests of Luz   Luz's tests   Luz's test's

8. the necklaces of Debbie   Debbie's necklaces'   Debbie's necklaces

9. the problems of Emily   Emily's problems   Emily problem's

10. the issues of the world   world issues'   world's issues

Commonly Confused Words

Some pairs of words sound or look very much alike. However, they do not have the same meanings. *Homonyms* are words with the same spelling and pronunciations but different meanings. Here are some examples:

Word	Meaning	Word	Meaning
bore	pest, nuisance (noun)	*lie*	falsehood (noun)
bore	caliber (noun)	*lie*	to tell a falsehood (verb)
bore	drill (verb)	*lie*	place down (verb)
bore	annoy (verb)		

Homophones are words with the same pronunciation but different spellings and meanings. Here are some examples:

Word	Meaning	Word	Meaning
heir	beneficiary	*hear*	listen
	atmosphere	*here*	in this place
err	make a mistake		

Twenty-five Often Confused Words

The following twenty-five word groups are often confused and misused.

1. *a lot*: many   *allot*: divide
2. *are*: form of "to be"   *our*: belonging to us
3. *brake*: device for slowing a vehicle   *break*: to crack or destroy
4. *buy*: to purchase   *by*: near or next to
5. *cell*: a small room, as in a prison   *sell*: to trade
6. *cent*: a penny   *scent*: smell
7. *cheep*: what a bird says   *cheap*: not expensive
8. *conscience*: moral sense   *conscious*: awake
9. *deer*: animal   *dear*: beloved
10. *dessert*: sweet at the end of a meal   *desert*: dry region

11. *do*: to act or make (verb)   *due*: caused by (adjective)

12. *dye*: change color   *die*: cease living

13. *here*: in this place   *hear*: to listen

14. *hole*: crater, opening   *whole*: entire

15. *hours*: 60 minutes   *ours*: belonging to us

16. *knew*: past tense of "to know"   *new*: not old

17. *lead*: bluish-gray metal   *led*: past tense of "to lead"

18. *maid*: a female servant   *made*: did

19. *meat*: animal flesh   *meet*: encounter; proper

20. *one*: 1, a single unit   *won*: past tense of "to win"

21. *passed*: past tense of "to pass"   *past*: gone by, ended, over

22. *peace*: calm   *piece*: section

23. *plain*: not beautiful; obvious   *plane*: airplane

24. *quiet*: not noisy   *quite*: almost

25. *to*: preposition (shows direction)   *two*: number   *too*: also

Quick Quiz C

Directions: Choose the words to complete each sentence in the following thank-you letter.

(1) During today's interview, I learned that (they're, there) (our, are) (a lot, allot) of different aspects to the trucking industry. (2) I thought I (knew, new) all about the business, but (it's, its) not as (plane, plain) as I thought. (3) I learned a little about how to (by, buy) and (cell, sell) equipment—especially that equipment is not (cheep, cheap)! (4) Thank you for spending an entire (our, hour) with me and teaching me a (hole, whole) lot. (5) I hope to (here, hear) from you soon.

Answers to Quick Quizzes

Answers to Quick Quiz A

1. wouldn't
2. you're
3. she'd
4. I'll
5. we'll
6. he's
7. there's
8. they're
9. you're
10. it's

Answers to Quick Quiz B

1. Bill's idea
2. Martha's pets
3. Charles' pencil
4. company's workers
5. Leslie's job
6. Michel's shoes
7. Luz's tests
8. Debbie's necklaces
9. Emily's problems
10. world's issues

Answers to Quick Quiz C

1. there, are, a lot
2. knew, it's, plain
3. buy, sell, cheap
4. hour, whole
5. hear

Practice Test

Directions: Choose the <u>one best answer</u> to each question.

Questions 1–5 refer to the following letter from the fire department.

(1) Two protect you're home against fire, you should first get a smoke detector. (2) They our sold in store's all over, cheep, and very easy to install. (3) Second, its' important to check all appliances four frayed cords and broken plugs. (4) By fire extinguishers for the kitchen; there easy to use. (5) Last, the mayor's office is handing out free fire safety maps so you can take your hole family on a safety drill.

1. Which correction should be made to sentence 1?

   (1) Replace <u>Two</u> with <u>Too</u>
   (2) Replace <u>Two</u> with <u>To</u>
   (3) Replace <u>Two</u> with <u>Too</u> and <u>you're</u> with <u>your</u>
   (4) Replace <u>you're</u> with <u>your</u>
   (5) Replace <u>Two</u> with <u>To</u> and <u>you're</u> with <u>your</u>

2. Which correction should be made to sentence 2?

   (1) Replace <u>our</u> with <u>are</u>, <u>store's</u> with <u>stores</u>, and <u>cheep</u> with <u>cheap</u>
   (2) Replace <u>our</u> with <u>are</u>, <u>store's</u> with <u>stores'</u>, and <u>cheep</u> with <u>cheap</u>
   (3) Replace <u>our</u> with <u>are</u> and <u>store's</u> with <u>stores's</u>
   (4) Replace <u>store's</u> with <u>stores</u>
   (5) Replace <u>cheep</u> with <u>cheap</u>

3. Which correction should be made to sentence 3?

   (1) Replace <u>its'</u> with <u>it's</u> and <u>to</u> with <u>two</u>
   (2) Replace <u>four</u> with <u>for</u>
   (3) Replace <u>its'</u> with <u>its</u> and <u>four</u> with <u>for</u>
   (4) Replace <u>its'</u> with <u>it's</u> and <u>four</u> with <u>for</u>
   (5) Replace <u>its'</u> with <u>it's</u> and <u>to</u> with <u>too</u>

4. Which correction should be made to sentence 4?

(1) Replace <u>to</u> with <u>too</u> and <u>extinguishers</u> with <u>extinguishers'</u>

(2) Replace <u>for</u> with <u>four</u> and <u>extinguishers</u> with <u>extinguisher's</u>

(3) Replace <u>by</u> with <u>buy</u> and <u>there</u> with <u>they're</u>

(4) Replace <u>by</u> with <u>buy</u> and <u>there</u> with <u>their</u>

(5) Replace <u>by</u> with <u>buy</u> and <u>to</u> with <u>two</u>

5. Which correction should be made to sentence 5?

(1) Replace <u>mayor's</u> with <u>mayors'</u> and <u>hole</u> with <u>whole</u>

(2) Replace <u>hole</u> with <u>whole</u>

(3) Replace <u>mayor's</u> with <u>mayors</u> and <u>hole</u> with <u>whole</u>

(4) Replace <u>maps</u> with <u>map's</u>

(5) Replace <u>maps</u> with <u>maps'</u> and <u>mayor's</u> with <u>mayors'</u>

Answers

1. **The correct answer is (5).**
2. **The correct answer is (1).**
3. **The correct answer is (4).**
4. **The correct answer is (3).**
5. **The correct answer is (2).**

The Language Arts, Writing Test

The Writing 12
Process

In the second part of the Language Arts, Writing Test, you will have to write an essay about an issue or a subject of general interest. You will be given a topic and must write on the assigned topic *only*. If you write on a different topic, you will not receive credit.

Successful writers usually follow a specific process when they write. Learning the steps in this process can help you write more easily and effectively.

Overview of the Writing Process

The writing process can be divided into three steps: *planning*, *drafting*, and *revising*. The following chart shows what each step means and how to spend the 45 minutes you will have on the GED to write your essay.

Step	Process	Time
planning	think of ideas	5 minutes
	arrange ideas into a rough outline	
drafting	write your first copy	20 minutes
	include details and examples	
Revising	correct mistakes	20 minutes
	add more details, if necessary	
	cut unnecessary information	
	make a clean copy, if time permits	

Let's look at each step in detail.

Step #1: Planning

When you plan, you think of ideas to include in your essay. This is often called "brainstorming." You can brainstorm in many ways. These include:

- Making a web or other graphic
- Listing subtopics
- Answering the questions: *Who? What? When? Where? Why? How?*

Before you do anything else, rephrase the writing prompt in your own words to make sure that you understand it. Remember: You will not receive any credit if you don't answer the question you are asked.

To make all of this make sense, you should make a "web." To do this, draw a circle in the middle of a sheet of paper. Add lines going out from the circle. At the end of each line, draw a circle and fill it in with a subtopic. Here is a sample web for an essay on the following GED writing prompt:

Suppose you had the opportunity to give someone a tour of your town. In your essay, identify what parts of the town you would tour and why. Use your experience and knowledge to support your essay.

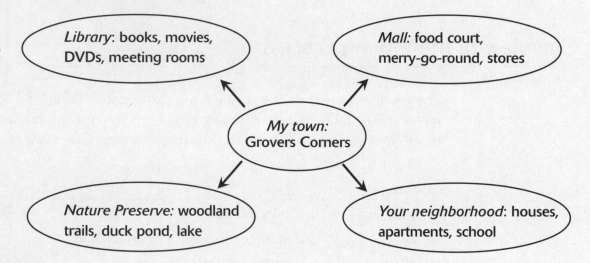

You do not have to use all these ideas in your essay. Perhaps you will only use two, one in each paragraph of the body. However, making a web helps you get your ideas down on paper. This gives you the choice of subtopics to use. Always choose the subtopics that will best answer the question and appeal to your reader.

Quick Quiz A

Directions: Make a web to generate ideas for the following GED essay:

Discuss an important lesson you learned. In your essay, explain the lesson you learned and how you learned it. Use your experience and knowledge to support your essay.

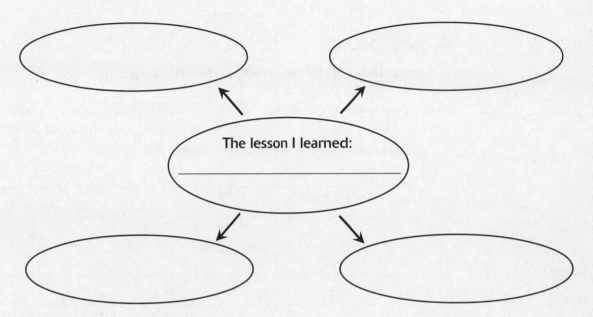

Step #2: Drafting

Follow these steps as you write your essay:

1. Be sure to write in ink. Your essay will not be accepted for credit if it is written in pencil.

2. Write in your test booklet. Only the writing in your test booklet will be scored. Any writing you do on scrap paper is for your use only. It will not be counted—even if you don't finish the essay.

3. It is natural to start your essay with the introduction, but if you are stuck for an opening, don't waste time. Instead, start where you can, even if it is in the middle. While it is important that your essay is well organized and logical, it is equally important that you get it written in the 45 minutes you have. The best essay in the world won't get you any points if you don't get it down on paper within the time limit.

4. Keep writing. If you get stuck, skip some lines and keep on writing. If you can't keep on writing, take a few deep breaths and gather your wits. If you are still stuck, move on to another part of the essay. Staring at the paper only wastes time.

5. Write neatly. If your writing cannot be read, the scorer won't be able to grade your paper. If it is messy, your scorer might misread a crucial point. If you know your handwriting is hard to read, print neatly and carefully.

6. Be focused, serious, and mature. Some people take the GED for them-selves and their future; others take it for their parents or other family members. A few people are forced to take it. If you didn't want to take the GED, this is not the time to throw the test to prove a point. If you are being forced to take the test, prove that you *can* do it.

7. Use a clock as you practice writing GED essays. This will teach you how to pace yourself so you can make sure that you finish the essay on the day of the test.

Quick Quiz B

Directions: Write an essay on the following topic:

Suppose you had the opportunity to give someone a tour of your town. In your essay, identify what parts of the town you would tour and why. Use your experience and knowledge to support your essay.

_____

_____

_____

_____

_____

_____

_____

_____

_____

_____

_____

_____

_____

_____

_____

_____

_____

_____

_____

_____

_____

_____

_____

_____

_____

_____

_____

_____

_____

_____

_____

_____

_____

_____

_____

_____

_____

Step #3: Revising

When you revise your essay, you do the following things:

- Correct mistakes in spelling, grammar, usage, punctuation, and capitalization
- Add more details, if necessary
- Cut unnecessary information
- Make a clean copy, if time permits

You will learn how to revise your essay in Chapter 15.

Quick Quiz C

Directions: Follow the three steps in the writing process with the following sample essay prompt. Write your essay at the end of this book or on a separate sheet of paper. Write in pen. Allow yourself 45 minutes.

Suppose you had the opportunity to learn something new. It might be a language, a science, or a physical skill. In your essay, identify what you would like to learn and explain why. Use your observations, experience, and knowledge to support your essay.

Assess Your Writing

You should always use this Essay Evaluation Checklist as you assess your writing. This is the same checklist you used in the Pretest. Make copies and fill out a checklist each time you write a practice essay.

Essay Evaluation Checklist

1. **Main Ideas**

   _____ Do my main points directly answer the question?

   _____ Are my main points persuasive and logical? Will they convince my readers that my point is valid?

   _____ Are my ideas linked in a logical way? Does my essay have unity?

2. **Organization**

   _____ Does my essay have a clear beginning that introduces my main points?

   _____ Does my essay have at least two body paragraphs? Do I start a new paragraph for each main point?

   _____ Does my essay have a conclusion that sums up my main points?

3. **Development of ideas**

   _____ Do I include specific details to make my point? (*Details* are examples, facts, statistics, reasons, definitions, and descriptions.)

   _____ Are my facts correct?

   _____ Do my details really prove my point?

4. **Skills**

   _____ Have I spelled all words correctly?

   _____ Have I used correct grammar?

   _____ Have I corrected all errors in punctuation and capitalization?

   _____ Can my handwriting be read easily? Have I written in pen?

Answers to Quick Quizzes

Answers to Quick Quiz A

Answers will vary.

Answers to Quick Quiz B

Answers will vary.

Answers to Quick Quiz C

Here is a sample essay:

[1] If I had the chance to learn a new skill, I would learn a foreign language. I never studied a foreign language in school, and I regret that choice. There are many reasons why a foreign language would be useful to me now. [2] First, it would help me communicate with my neighbors. [3] Second, and perhaps more important, it would help me get a job.

[4] I live in a neighborhood with many Spanish-speaking people. [5] Many of my neighbors are newcomers to America from Mexico, Puerto Rico, Colombia, and El Salvador. We try to help each other in many ways, but it is often hard to communicate because I do not know Spanish. [5] For example, my neighbor Fred Ruiz is a plumber. Last week, he tried to teach me how to repair a broken pipe under my kitchen sink. It took the whole day for Fred to teach me how to fix the pipe because we could not communicate easily. [7] If I knew Spanish, I would have learned much more easily.

[8] Knowing a second language would make my job search easier, too. Last week I applied for a job at a pharmacy as a clerk. [9] The manager said, "Many of our customers speak foreign languages. We are looking for clerks who are bilingual. Do you speak a second language?" Since I do not speak another language, I did not qualify for the job. [10] The local bank, supermarket, and clothing stores are also looking for people who speak foreign languages as well as English. [11] Someday, I want to be a police officer. I spoke with the police department. The officer in charge told me that knowing a second language would help me get a job with the police. It would also help me as a police officer. [12] These experiences showed me the advantages of knowing a foreign language.

[13] I wish I had studied a second language in school, because it would help me now. [14] I would be able to communicate with my neighbors more easily, and I would be able to qualify for more jobs. Fortunately, it is never too late to learn. After I pass my GED, I am going to enroll in Spanish classes at the local evening school.

Explanation

[1] Topic sentence answers the question

[2] First main point

[3] Second main point

[4] First main point

[5] Details

[6] Example

[7] Writer makes the point

[8] Second-most important idea

[9] Example

[10] Details

[11] Example

[12] Writer makes the point

[13] Conclusion restates the main idea

[14] Summarizes two main points

Practice Test

At the end of this book or on a separate sheet of paper, write the following essay. Make sure you use the writing process. After you've finished, use the Essay Evaluation Checklist. You should ask a teacher or someone whose writing you admire to read your essay.

If you could have three wishes, what would they be and why? Use your personal observations, experience, and knowledge to support your ideas.

Answers

Essays will vary.

Patterns of Organization 13

Your essay on the GED Language Arts, Writing Test should be about 200 to 400 words long. It should have four to five paragraphs. There are many ways to organize your essay. In this chapter, you will learn several ways. On the day of the test, choose the way that you are most comfortable with.

Order of Paragraphs

When writing an essay, it is important to consider the importance of each of your points as it relates to the main idea. It is then necessary to decide the order in which you will present your points. Many essays begin with the most important point and end with the least important points. With this kind of organization, put your most important point first. Then add your second-most important point. End with your weakest point. The essay would be arranged like this:

Most-to-Least Important Points
Paragraph #1   Introduction
Paragraph #2   Most important point
Paragraph #3   Second-most important point
Paragraph #4   Least important point
Paragraph #5   Conclusion

You could also arrange your ideas from least to most important, or save the second-most important point for last.

Least-to-Most Important Points
Paragraph #1   Introduction
Paragraph #2   Least important point
Paragraph #3   Second-most important point
Paragraph #4   Most important point
Paragraph #5   Conclusion

Most-Least-Second-Most Important Points

Paragraph #1   Introduction
Paragraph #2   Most important point
Paragraph #3   Least important point
Paragraph #4   Second-most important point
Paragraph #5   Conclusion

There is no right or wrong order of paragraphs. Choose the order that you are most comfortable with.

Quick Quiz A

Directions: Write an essay on the following topic. First, arrange your points from most important to least important.

Why do students fail in school? In your essay, identify the reasons why students fail. Use your personal observations, experience, and knowledge to support your ideas.

First, complete this outline to show how you will arrange your points.

Paragraph #1   _____

Paragraph #2   _____

Paragraph #3   _____

Paragraph #4   _____

Paragraph #5   _____

Now, write the essay. As you write, follow your outline and your order of paragraphs.

_____

_____

_____

_____

_____

_____

_____

_____

_____

_____

_____

Chronological Order

With this organizational plan, you arrange your ideas in time order. This is the order in which they happened, from first to last. This is a very good method of organization if you are telling a story.

Use a timeline like the one below to help you order events. Include as many events as you need. Usually, you will have three to four events.

First event → Second event → Third event → Last event/Conclusion

---

Chronological essays often include *transitions* that help readers track the order of events according to the time in which they happened. These *time-order transitions* are words that include actual dates, including days of the week, months, and years. In addition, you can use the following clue words:

Time-order Transitions			
after	at that time	finally	first, second, etc.
last	later	next	now
subsequently	succeeding	soon after	then

Quick Quiz B

Directions: Write an essay on the following topic. Arrange your points in chronological order, from the beginning to the end of the story.

If you could go back and change one mistake in your life, what would it be? In your essay, tell about the mistake and why you would change it. Use your personal observations, experience, and knowledge to support your ideas.

First, complete this timeline to show how you will arrange your points.

First event → Second event → Third event → Last event/Conclusion

---

Now, write your essay. As you write, use chronological order.

_____

_____

_____

_____

_____

Answers to Quick Quizzes

Possible Answers to Quick Quiz A

Paragraph #1   Introduction

Paragraph #2   Most important point: *Students fail because they don't try hard enough.*

Paragraph #3   Second-most important point: *Students fail because of dull subjects.*

Paragraph #4   Least important point: *Students fail because of poor teaching.*

Paragraph #5   Conclusion

Here is a sample essay. Notice how the writer gives a lot of details to support the three main ideas.

[1] There are three main reasons why students fail in school. [2] First and most important, students do poorly in school because they do not try hard enough. [3] Second, students fail because the subjects are dull. [4] Last, students fail because of poor teaching. I saw all this when I was in high school.

[5] Most important, too many students refuse to take responsibility for their actions. They often say, "It's not my fault; the teacher doesn't know how to teach," or "The class is so boring that you can't expect me to pay attention." Instead, students should say, "It's my fault because I didn't study enough" or "I should have turned off the hockey game and opened up the textbook." Sometimes, you will get a teacher who isn't that good or a subject that is boring to you. But that's no excuse. You have to deal with it and take charge of your own future.

[6] Second, students fail because of dull subjects. I always found math and science really boring. I did not earn good grades in Earth Science because I could not get interested in clouds and weather. My friend Stu actually fell asleep in history class because he found ancient history so boring! However, I really liked math and wood shop. It was fun to work with shapes in geometry and build flower boxes in shop. If all my classes were that interesting, I know I would have done better in school.

[7] Finally, students fail because of poor teaching. Some teachers are really good. They get their students really involved in the class. Unfortunately, a lot of teachers cannot teach well. My 9th-grade English teacher just stood in front of the room and read from the textbook. She

never even asked us any questions about it. My 10th-grade math teacher gave us lots and lots of problems to solve. Half the class did not do the work. Students learn more when teachers are interesting. Then they are less likely to fail.

[8] Succeeding in school is important. It is often a big factor in your future. So when students fail in high school, we can place the blame where it belongs: on their shoulders. However, some students fail because the work is boring to them. Finally, students fail because of weak teaching. My friends and I had trouble in school because of all three factors, so I know their importance.

Explanation

[1] Topic sentence

[2] Most important idea introduced

[3] Second-most important idea introduced

[4] Least important idea introduced

[5] Most important idea proven

[6] Second-most important idea proven

[7] Least important idea proven

[8] Conclusion

Answers to Quick Quiz B

Possible Timeline:

| buy the fireworks | go to Mark's house | set off fireworks | Fireworks explode/ Jon is seriously hurt |

First event   →   Second event   →   Third event   →   Last event/conclusion

Here is a sample essay:

Everyone makes mistakes. Some mistakes aren't too important, like wearing the wrong clothes to a big party or forgetting to take out the trash. Other mistakes, however, can have a big effect on your life. I made a big mistake when I was 16 years old. **[1]** If I could go back and change that event, I would.

[2] It was July 4th. Like all the other kids on our block, we wanted fireworks. July 4th wasn't any fun without fireworks, we thought. We put all our money together. We had a lot of money—nearly $100. We went down to the truck on the turnpike and bought a big load of fireworks. We got really powerful ones, too. They weren't little sparklers or caps. That was the first part of our mistake.

[3] The second part of our mistake was taking the fireworks to Mark's house. His house was far away from town. It was far from other houses, too. There were no neighbors close by. Mark's parents were never home. There was no one close by to help us if needed.

[4] We started setting off the fireworks. It was a lot of fun because they were so bright and colorful. The sky seemed to explode with streaks of red, blue, silver, and gold. The fireworks made loud noises. Boom! Boom! Boom! they went. We laughed a lot that night, until Jon set off a really big fireworks. He lit the fuse, but the fireworks was a dud. When it did not go off, he ran back to get it. Just as he reached down, the fireworks exploded. All of a sudden, Jon was covered in blood.

[5] We took Jon to the hospital as fast as we could. We were far away from the center of town so it took a long time. The doctors worked very hard, but Jon's eyesight was permanently damaged. I wish we had never bought all those fireworks. I wish someone had been home to help us when we set off the fireworks. Maybe then Jon would be well now.

Explanation

[1] Topic sentence

[2] First event

[3] Second Event

[4] Third Event

[5] Last event/conclusion

Practice Test

At the end of this book or on separate sheets of paper, write the following essays. Use order of paragraphs or chronological order. Remember to use your Essay Evaluation Guide when you've written your essays. Ask a teacher or someone else whose writing you admire to read your essays.

Essay 1

How could you make the world a better place? In your essay, describe what you would like to improve in the world and how you would go about doing it. Use your personal observations, experience, and knowledge to support your ideas.

Essay 2

Who has had an important influence on your life? In your essay, identify the person who has had a big influence on your life and tell why. Use your personal observations, experience, and knowledge to support your ideas.

Answers

Essays will vary.

Using Specific Details 14

Details are small pieces of information that support the main idea. Details answer the questions *who, what, when, where, which,* and *how*. Details tell about people, events, things, time, objects, situations, or the way something happened.

Why Use Details?

Without details, your writing is flat and dull. It does not tell your readers what they need and want to know. Use details to

- Make your writing more specific and vivid. Details help readers visualize your topic and main idea.
- Make your writing more precise. Details help you prevent misunderstandings.
- Make your writing interesting. Details add color and flavor to your writing.

Types of Details

Details can be divided into six main categories:

1. **Examples:** *Examples* are models that are used to illustrate a writer's point. Examples help a reader understand a general statement by giving specific information that represents one piece of the whole concept.

2. **Facts:** *Facts* are statements that can be proven.

3. **Statistics:** *Statistics* are numbers used to give additional information.

4. **Reasons:** *Reasons* are explanations. They tell *why* something happened.

5. **Definitions:** *Definitions* are statements that explain what something means. Definitions often come from the dictionary.

6. **Descriptions:** *Descriptions* are words or phrases that tell *how* something looks, smells, tastes, sounds, or feels. Descriptions help readers visualize or get a mental picture of what they are reading.

Below are examples of each type of detail:

Types of Details	Examples
Examples	Many famous people come from Long Island. For example, the poet Walt Whitman, the singer Billy Joel, and the comedian Jerry Seinfeld all lived on Long Island.
Facts	Tulsa is a city in Oklahoma.
Statistics (numbers)	Florida has 105 state parks with a total of 215,820 acres.
Reasons	Many people visit Washington, DC, to see its grand buildings and historic sites.
Definitions	The name *Florida* comes from a Spanish word that means "feast of flowers."
Descriptions	The naughty cat scratched the tattered green sofa.

Make Details Specific

When you write your details, be as specific as you can. Name particular people, places, and things. Use proper nouns rather than common nouns. For example, write *Cher* rather than *a singer, Golden Gate Bridge* rather than *a bridge,* and *Thanksgiving* rather than *a holiday.* In the same way, write an exact number rather than *some, a few, several,* or *many.*

Quick Quiz A

Directions: Circle the most specific detail in each line.

1. man	President George Bush
2. the Midwest	Dayton, Ohio
3. some eggs	four eggs
4. bright color	cherry red
5. flower	tulip

Directions: Write a specific detail for each category.

6. late   _____

7. television show   _____

8. friend   _____

9. color   _____

10. place   _____

Quick Quiz B

Directions: Read the passage and fill out the chart that follows. You may wish to underline the details as you read to make them easier to find.

Levi Strauss invented blue jeans by a sudden brainstorm. In 1850, 21-year-old Levi Strauss traveled from New York to San Francisco. He took needles, thread, pots, pans, ribbons, yarn, scissors, buttons, and canvas across the country to sell to the gold miners. The small items sold well, but Strauss found himself stuck with the rolls of canvas because it was not heavy enough to be used for tents.

While talking to one of the miners, Strauss learned that it was hard to find sturdy pants. On the spot, Strauss measured the man with a piece of string. For six dollars in gold dust, Strauss had a piece of the left-over canvas made into a pair of stiff but rugged pants. The miner was delighted with the results, and word got around about "Levi's pants."

Business was so good that Levi Strauss was soon out of canvas. He wrote to his two brothers in New York to send more. He received instead a tough brown cotton cloth made in Nimes, France, called *serge de Nimes*. Almost at once, the foreign term was shortened to *denim*. Strauss had the cloth dyed a rich blue called "indigo," which became a company trademark. These were the humble beginnings of a fashion that would take the world by storm.

Examples: _____

_____

Facts: _____

_____

Statistics (numbers): _____

_____

Reasons: _____

_____

Definitions: _____

_____

Descriptions: _____

_____

Answers to Quick Quizzes

Answers to Quick Quiz A

1. President George Bush
2. Dayton, Ohio
3. four eggs
4. cherry red
5. tulip

Note: Answers will vary. Here are some sample answers:

6. 10:00 P.M.
7. The Simpsons
8. Cecilia Vaca
9. dark green
10. Jones Beach, Field 6

Possible Answers to Quick Quiz B

Examples: He took needles, thread, pots, pans, ribbons, yarn, scissors, buttons, and canvas across the country to sell to the gold miners.

Facts: In 1850, 21-year-old Levi Strauss traveled from New York to San Francisco.

Statistics (numbers): For six dollars in gold dust (...)

Reasons: Business was so good that Levi Strauss was soon out of canvas.

Definitions: He received instead a tough brown cotton cloth made in Nimes, France, called *serge de Nimes*. The foreign term was shortened to *denim*.

Descriptions: Strauss found himself stuck with the rolls of canvas because it was not heavy enough to be used for tents. On the spot, Strauss measured the man with a piece of string.

Practice Test

Directions: Choose the one best answer to each question.

Questions 1–5 refer to the following paragraph.

(1) Juliette Gordon Low started the Girl Scouts of America. (2) When she died in 1927, there were 168,000 Girl Scouts in the United States. (3) Today, there are more girls involved in Scouting on all levels. (4) Girl Scouts from everywhere in the United States can meet other Girl Scouts at two special places called "national centers." (5) The Juliette Gordon Low Girl Scout National Center is the home in Savannah, Georgia, where Juliette Gordon Low was born. (6) The other national center for Girl Scouts to meet is the Edith Macy Conference Center. (7) Adults—not children—meet there to learn more about Girl Scouts.

1. Which revision would improve the effectiveness of sentence 1?

    (1) Replace Juliette Gordon Low with She

    (2) Replace Juliette Gordon Low with A woman

    (3) Add in the past after America

    (4) Add in 1912 after America

    (5) Add a long time ago after America

2. How many girls were involved in scouting when Juliette Gordon Low died?

    (1) 168,000 girls

    (2) Fewer than 200,000 girls

    (3) More than 200,000 girls

    (4) More than a million girls

    (5) Some

3. Which revision would improve the effectiveness of sentence 3?

    (1) Add many after more

    (2) Delete Today

    (3) Add than 200,000 after more

    (4) Replace Today with Now

    (5) Add a lot before more

4. Which revision would improve the effectiveness of sentence 5?

(1) Cut in Savannah, Georgia,

(2) Add , also known as "The Birthplace," after Center

(3) Replace Savannah, Georgia, with the South

(4) Replace Juliette Gordon Low Girl Scout National Center with the place

(5) Cut where Juliette Gordon Low was born

5. Which revision would improve the effectiveness of sentence 6?

(1) Cut for Girl Scouts to meet

(2) Add in Briarcliff Manor, New York after Center

(3) Cut Edith Macy

(4) Replace national with big

(5) Cut national center

6. Who visits the Edith Macy Conference Center to learn more about Girl Scouts?

(1) Girl Scout troops

(2) Edith Macy

(3) Individual Girl Scouts

(4) Children from all over the United States

(5) Adults

Answers

1. **The correct answer is (4).** The date is a specific detail that makes the sentence more precise and descriptive. None of the other choices adds details.

2. **The correct answer is (1).** The statistic makes the sentence more specific.

3. **The correct answer is (3).** Adding the statistic makes the sentence more specific. None of the other choices adds details.

4. **The correct answer is (2).** The phrase <u>, also known as "The Birthplace,"</u> is a specific detail that makes the writing more precise.

5. **The correct answer is (2).** The phrase <u>in Briarcliff Manor, New York</u> is a specific detail that makes the writing more precise.

6. **The correct answer is (5).** The answer is directly stated in sentence 7: <u>Adults—not children—meet there to learn more about Girl Scouts.</u>

Revising and Proofreading | 15

Revising and proofreading help you improve your writing. When you *revise,* you make sure that all the words in your essay are spelled correctly. You check for problems with grammar, punctuation, and usage, too. But revising is much more than checking for mistakes in writing skills.

Revising is also about trying different ideas to get your point across clearly and smoothly. When you revise, you *elaborate* on ideas by adding any new information that you need. You also *cut out* ideas and details that don't fit. You can *reword* sentences, too. This helps make your writing smoother and more logical. That way, readers will better understand what you are saying.

Guidelines for Revising

As you begin to revise your essay, think about your *audience* and *purpose* for writing.

- Your *audience* is the people who will read your essay. Here, your audience is GED scorers. To meet their needs, ask yourself, "What does my audience know about my topic? What information do I have to give to make my paper clear?"

- Your *purpose* is your reason for writing. To find the purpose, ask yourself, "What am I trying to accomplish in my essay?" On the GED Language Arts, Writing Test, your purpose will be to explain an issue or prove a point. Sometimes, you will do both.

Quick Quiz A

Directions: Read the following sample GED writing prompt. Then answer the questions that follow.

Choose a situation in your life when you realized that you had to do something because there was no one else who could or would do it. In your essay, describe what you had to do and explain why. Use your personal observations, experiences, and knowledge to support your essay.

1. My audience is _____

2. My purpose is _____

Revise by Elaboration

Elaboration is adding details to support your main idea. You learned all about details in Chapter 14. Details, facts, definitions, examples, statistics, and quotations are types of elaboration you can use. Elaboration makes your writing more interesting as well as more complete.

Below is the first draft of an essay. As you read the draft, think about some other questions you might have about the topic.

The color barrier that had kept major league sports white-only did not fall in baseball until a manager brought up Jackie Robinson from the minor leagues. Facing down hostility and prejudice, Robinson was named Rookie of the Year. The way was opened for black athletes who have since enriched professional sports. Nonetheless, it was not until years later that an African American became the coach of a major United States team. The man was Bill Russell. In 1968 and 1969, his team won the NBA championship.

Here is how the writer elaborated. The details are underlined. As you read, notice how the facts, examples, and statistics make the writing clearer. These details help the writer follow the GED instructions to include "specific development of your ideas."

The color barrier that had kept major league sports white-only did not fall in baseball until <u>1947</u>, when <u>Branch Rickey</u> <u>of the Brooklyn Dodgers</u> brought up Jackie Robinson from the minor leagues. Facing down hostility and prejudice <u>with dignity and superb playing,</u> Robinson was named Rookie of the Year. The way was opened for black athletes who have since enriched professional sports. Nonetheless, it was not until <u>1966</u> that an African American became the coach of a major United States

professional sports team. The man was Bill Russell, <u>and the team was
the Boston Celtics of the National Basketball Association.</u> In 1968 and
1969, <u>the Celtics</u> won the NBA championship <u>with Russell as player-
coach. As a full-time player, the six-foot-nine-inch center led the Celtics
to eight straight NBA championships from 1959 to 1966. He was voted
the league's most valuable player five times.</u>

Quick Quiz B

Directions: Revise the following paragraph by adding elaboration. Draw
your details from the list. Then rewrite the passage on the lines. Be ready to
explain your choices.

Given by the people of France to the people of the United States as a
symbol of freedom and friendship, the Statue of Liberty is the largest
freestanding sculpture ever created. The statue has an interior framework of iron that keeps it from toppling over.

Details
It weighs 450,000 pounds and rises 151 feet above its pedestal.
Ms. Liberty boasts eyes two and a half feet wide.
The Statue's mouth is three feet wide.
Its nose is four and a half feet long. Her upraised right arm extends forty-two feet; her hand is nearly seventeen feet long.
Her fingers are close to ten feet long.

_____

_____

_____

_____

_____

_____

_____

Revise by Cutting

When you cut, you get rid of information that is off the topic. You also get rid of information that repeats what has already been said. Study this chart for guidelines:

Problem	Solution
Saying something twice	Cut the unnecessary word or words
Bring the project to <u>final</u> completion.	*Bring the project to completion.*
Adding meaningless words	Cut the empty phrases
<u>*The point that I am trying to make is that*</u> *reporters should not invade people's privacy.*	*Reporters should not invade people's privacy.*
Using several words when one is better	Cut the extra words
The <u>big, huge, massive</u> cloud covered the sun.	*The massive cloud covered the sun.*
Starting sentences with "It" or "There"	Start with the subject.
<u>*There were*</u> *dogs barking in the alley.*	*Dogs barked in the alley.*

Quick Quiz C

Directions: Revise the following paragraph by cutting any unnecessary details. Then rewrite the passage on the lines. Be ready to explain each cut you made.

(1) Researchers interviewed and talked with more than two hundred people who have experienced problems with high school. (2) The researchers wanted to find out why some smart people fail, bomb, and fall short at high school, while others succeed. (3) The results show that in a very real sense many people don't understand that high school success often involves studying hard. (4) There are many students who claim that conflicts with their teachers caused their problems. (5) In point of fact, however, many students fail because they are not committed to their education.

_____

_____

_____

_____

_____

Revise by Rewording

Often, you will have to replace words and revise sentences to make your writing accurate and fresh. Start by looking for words that are overused. Follow these suggestions:

1. Replace overused adjectives such as excellent, good, and nice with vivid words.

2. Use specific nouns rather than general nouns such as stuff and things.

3. Replace repeated nouns (especially names) with pronouns. Use he, she, or it for repeated names.

4. Substitute other repeated words with synonyms, words that mean the same thing.

5. Make sure your writing has words that appeal to the five senses: sight, sound, taste, touch, and smell.

Here's an example of revising by rewording.

(1) In 1869, Antonio Lopez de Santa Anna, the excellent Mexican leader of the Alamo attack, went into exile on Staten Island, New York. (2) Santa Anna had brought stuff with him. (3) Santa Anna wasn't interested in chewing the stuff; instead, he hoped it could become a substitute for rubber.

(1) Cross out <u>excellent</u>. Replace with *celebrated*

(2) Replace <u>stuff</u> with *a large lump of chicle.*

(3) Replace <u>Santa Anna</u> with *He*

(4) Replace <u>stuff</u> with *sticky substance*

(1) In 1869, Antonio Lopez de Santa Anna, the celebrated Mexican leader of the Alamo attack, went into exile on Staten Island, New York. (2) Santa Anna had brought a large lump of chicle with him. (3) He wasn't interested in chewing the sticky substance; instead, he hoped it could become a substitute for rubber.

Quick Quiz D

Directions: Replace each underlined word in the following passage with a more vivid or exciting and accurate word. Be ready to explain each word change you made.

Adams was <u>going</u> down the street one day when he saw a small child buying a wax called "paraffin" at a <u>store</u>. This gave Adams a great idea. <u>Adams</u> asked the pharmacy manager if he would sell a new kind of gum. <u>The man</u> agreed. <u>Going</u> home, Adams <u>put</u> the chicle in water until it was soft. Then he <u>made</u> the chicle into little round shapes. They were a <u>dull</u> color, but every single ball of "gum" sold the very next day. With his profits, Adams went into business producing Adams New York Gum.

Answers to Quick Quizzes

Answers to Quick Quiz A

1. Your audience is GED scorers. They are adults who are trained to score essays.

2. Your purpose is to explain what you did and why.

Possible Answers to Quick Quiz B

Given by the people of France to the people of the United States as a symbol of freedom and friendship, the Statue of Liberty is the largest freestanding sculpture ever created. It weighs 450,000 pounds and rises 151 feet above its pedestal. Ms. Liberty boasts eyes two and a half feet wide. The statue's mouth is three feet wide. Its nose is four and a half feet long. Her upraised right arm extends forty-two feet; her hand is nearly seventeen feet long. Her fingers are close to ten feet long. The statue has an interior framework of iron that keeps it from toppling over.

Possible Answers to Quick Quiz C

(1) Researchers interviewed more than two hundred people who have experienced problems with high school. (2) The researchers wanted to find out why some smart people fail at high school, while others succeed. (3) The results show that many people don't understand that high school success often involves studying hard. (4) Many students claimed that conflicts with their teachers caused their problems. (5) However, many students fail because they are not committed to their education.

Possible Answers to Quick Quiz D

Adams was <u>jogging</u> down the street one day when he saw a small child buying a wax called "paraffin" at a <u>pharmacy</u>. This gave Adams a great idea. <u>He</u> asked the pharmacy manager if he would sell a new kind of gum. The <u>pharmacist</u> agreed. <u>Dashing</u> home, Adams <u>immersed</u> the chicle in water until it was soft. Then he <u>squeezed and</u> <u>pressed</u> the chicle into little round shapes. They were a <u>drab gray</u> color, but every single ball of "gum" sold the very next day. With his profits, Adams went into business producing Adams New York Gum.

Practice Test

Directions: At the end of this book or on separate sheets of paper, write the following essay. Be sure to revise and proofread your essay. Remember to use your Essay Evaluation Guide after completing your essay. Ask a teacher or someone else whose writing you admire to read your essay.

If you could have any career at all, what would it be and why? In your essay, identify the career you would like and explain why you want it. Use your personal observations, experience, and knowledge to support your ideas.

Answers

Essays will vary.

Reevaluating Your Skills

Posttest

Organization

Directions: Choose the one best answer to each question.

Questions 1–5 refer to the following part of a letter:

(1) First of all, head librarian Erika Saviuk always helps me find reference material. (2) Assistant clerk Val Jones arranges the rooms we use for our book club meetings. (3) Erika is very knowledgeable and professional. (4) My husband Herman doesn't like to read; he prefers to watch television. (5) Last but not least, the children's librarian Bob Schaeffer helps my children choose good books to read. (6) I enjoy coming to the library and recommend it to all my friends.

1. Which sentence would be most effective at the beginning of this paragraph?

   (1) Mark Brody keeps the sidewalks clean of snow.

   (2) I am writing this letter to compliment your excellent staff.

   (3) Ka-Po Chan does beautiful crafts for holidays.

   (4) Agnes and I come to the library every week.

   (5) People should use the library more often.

2. Which revision would improve the effectiveness of this letter?

   (1) Switch sentences 2 and 3

   (2) Delete sentence 3

   (3) Switch sentences 3 and 4

   (4) Switch sentences 4 and 5

   (5) Delete sentence 5

169

3. Sentence 2: **Assistant clerk Val Jones arranges the rooms we use for our book club meetings.**

What transition can be added to sentence 2?

(1) Before,

(2) Second,

(3) As a result,

(4) If,

(5) Nevertheless,

4. Which sentence is off the topic?

(1) Sentence 1

(2) Sentence 2

(3) Sentence 3

(4) Sentence 4

(5) Sentence 5

5. Which sentence best concludes this letter?

(1) In conclusion, your excellent staff makes the Springdale Public Library a great community resource!

(2) Hartsdale Library also has an excellent staff but they are not as friendly as your staff.

(3) The books I get at the library help me study for my GED, and they help me learn about the world.

(4) Luiz Munoz left your staff last year to take a job in another library.

(5) I got my first library card when I moved to this town.

Essay

Directions: At the end of this book or on separate sheets of paper, write the following essay. Be sure to revise and proofread your essay. Use the Essay Evaluation Guide at the end of this posttest when you've written your essay.

Whom do you admire as a modern-day hero? In your essay, identify the person you admire and explain why you consider this person heroic. The person may be a famous public figure, but does not have to be. Use your personal observations, experience, and knowledge to support your ideas.

Sentence Structure

Directions: Choose the <u>one best answer</u> to each question.

Questions 1–5 refer to the following paragraph.

(1) All returns must be made within 14 days merchandise must have a receipt. (2) You must make sure that all original tags attached. (3) Walking into the store, a refund desk is seen. (4) Customers will be referred to a help desk with a problem. (5) Customers should check in, take a number, and they should be waiting in line for the next available clerk.

1. Sentence 1: **All returns must be made within 14 <u>days merchandise</u> must have a receipt.**

    Which correction should be made to the underlined portion of this sentence?

    (1) No change
    (2) days, merchandise
    (3) days, and merchandise
    (4) days, since merchandise
    (5) days. Merchandise

2. Sentence 2: **You must make sure that all original <u>tags attached</u>**.

    Which correction should be made to the underlined portion of this sentence?

    (1) No change
    (2) tags attaching
    (3) tags was attached
    (4) tags attach
    (5) tags are attached

3. Sentence 3: <u>**Walking into the store, a refund desk is seen**</u>.

    Which is the best revision of sentence 3?

    (1) No change
    (2) A refund desk is seen walking into the store.
    (3) Walking into the store, a refund desk is easily seen.
    (4) Walking into the store, a refund desk can be seen.
    (5) As they walk into the store, customers will see a refund desk.

4. Sentence 4: <u>**Customers will be referred to a help desk with a problem**</u>.

Which is the best revision of sentence 4?

(1) No change

(2) Customers with a problem will be referred to a help desk.

(3) Customers with a help desk will be referred to a problem.

(4) Customers will be referring to a help desk with a problem.

(5) A help desk with a problem will refer to customers.

5. Sentence 5: **Customers should check in, take a number, and <u>they should be waiting in line</u> for the next available clerk.**

Which correction should be made to the underlined portion of sentence 4?

(1) No change

(2) wait in line

(3) they should have waited in line

(4) waiting in line

(5) waited in line

Essay

Directions: At the end of this book or on separate sheets of paper, write the following essay. Be sure to revise and proofread your essay. Use the Essay Evaluation Guide at the end of this posttest after you've written your essay.

Suppose you had the chance to have a special power. In your essay, identify the power and explain why you want it. Use your personal observations, experience, and knowledge to support your ideas.

Usage

Directions: Choose the <u>one best answer</u> to each question.

Questions 1–5 refer to the following paragraph.

(1) Dr. Roberts and Ms. Harris has agreed to give a class on time management. (2) All employees is invited to attend and lunch will be served. (3) You learns best by practicing, so you will get a calendar and date book to use. (4) Acceptance cards were gived out last week, and since space is limited, please return your card by Monday. (5) We hope this class can be attended by you.

1. Sentence 1: **Dr. Roberts and Ms. Harris has agreed to give a class on time management**.

   Which correction should be made to sentence 1?

   (1) Change <u>has</u> to <u>is</u>

   (2) Change <u>has</u> to <u>was</u>

   (3) Change <u>has</u> to <u>will have</u>

   (4) Change <u>has</u> to <u>gives</u>

   (5) Change <u>has</u> to <u>have</u>

2. Sentence 2: **All employees <u>is</u> invited to attend.**

   Which is the best way to write the underlined portion of this sentence?

   (1) No change

   (2) was

   (3) are

   (4) has

   (5) has been

3. Sentence 3: **You learns best by practicing, so you will get a calendar and date book.**

   Which correction should be made to sentence 3?

   (1) Change <u>learns</u> to <u>learning</u>

   (2) Change <u>learns</u> to <u>learn</u>

   (3) Change <u>learns</u> to <u>are learns</u>

   (4) Change <u>get</u> to <u>gets</u>

   (5) Change <u>get</u> to <u>getting</u>

4. Sentence 4: **Acceptance cards <u>were gived</u> out last week, and since space is limited, please return your card by Monday.**

Which is the best way to write the underlined portion of this sentence?

(1) No change

(2) were given

(3) were gaved

(4) give

(5) are given

5. Sentence 5: **We hope this class can be attended by you.**

Which is the best way to revise this sentence?

(1) We are hoping this class can be attended by you.

(2) We hope can be attended by you this class.

(3) We hope you this class can be attending.

(4) We hope you can attend this class.

(5) This class can be attended by you, we are hoping.

Essay

Directions: At the end of this book or on separate sheets of paper, write the following essay. Be sure to revise and proofread your essay. Use the Essay Evaluation Guide at the end of this posttest after you've written your essay.

If you could change places with anyone for a day, with whom would you switch places and why? In your essay, identify the person you would like to be for a day and explain why you chose this person. Use your personal observations, experience, and knowledge to support your ideas.

Mechanics

Directions: Choose the <u>one best answer</u> to each question.

Questions 1–5 refer to the following letter.

(1) on march 15 we received your loan application. (2) You're application will be processed quickly because its very important to us. (3) If you have any questions, please call luisa hernandez at the bank. (4) She is available Monday–Friday 9:00–5:00 she can also be reached Saturday mornings at the bank. (5) The banks officers try to help our customers.

1. Sentence 1: <u>**on march 15**</u> **we received your loan application.**

    Which is the best way to write the underlined portion of this sentence?

    (1) No change

    (2) On march 15

    (3) On March, 15

    (4) on March 15

    (5) On March 15,

2. Sentence 2: **You're application will be processed quickly because its very important to us.**

    Which correction(s) should be made to sentence 2?

    (1) Replace <u>you're</u> with <u>your'e</u>

    (2) Replace <u>you're</u> with <u>your</u> and <u>its</u> with <u>it's</u>

    (3) Replace <u>its</u> with <u>its'</u>

    (4) Replaced <u>its</u> with <u>I'ts</u>

    (5) Replace <u>you're</u> with <u>your</u> and <u>its</u> with <u>its'</u>

3. Sentence 3: **If you have any questions, please call luisa hernandez at the bank**.

    Which correction should be made to sentence 3?

    (1) Replace <u>luisa hernandez</u> with <u>Luisa hernandez</u>

    (2) Replace <u>luisa hernandez</u> with <u>luisa Hernandez</u>

    (3) Replace <u>luisa hernandez</u> with <u>Luisa Hernandez</u>

    (4) Replace <u>the bank</u> with <u>The Bank</u>

    (5) Replace <u>the bank</u> with <u>the Bank</u>

4. Sentence 4: **She is available Monday–Friday 9:00–5:00 she can also be reached Saturday mornings at the bank.**

   Which correction should be made to sentence 4?

   (1) Insert a comma after <u>5:00</u>

   (2) Insert a semicolon after <u>also</u>

   (3) Insert a semicolon after <u>reached</u>

   (4) Insert a semicolon after <u>5:00</u>

   (5) Replace <u>be reached</u> with <u>reaching</u>

5. Sentence 5: **The banks officers try to help our customers.**

   Which correction should be made to sentence 5?

   (1) Change <u>officers</u> to <u>officer's</u>

   (2) Change <u>banks</u> to <u>bank's</u>

   (3) Change <u>customers</u> to <u>customer's</u>

   (4) Change <u>customers</u> to <u>customers'</u>

   (5) Change <u>banks</u> to <u>banks's</u>

Essay

Directions: At the end of this book or on separate sheets of paper, write the following essay. Be sure to revise and proofread your essay. Use the Essay Evaluation Guide at the end of this posttest after you've written your essay.

What qualities make someone a good friend? In your essay, identify at least two qualities you look for in a friend. Tell about people you know who have these qualities. Use your personal observations, experience, and knowledge to support your ideas.

The Writing Test

Directions: At the end of this book or on separate sheets of paper, write the following essay. Be sure to revise and proofread your essay. Use the Essay Evaluation Guide at the end of this posttest after you've written your essay.

Is TV good or bad for children? In your essay, argue that television is good or bad for children. Use your personal observations, experience, and knowledge to support your ideas.

Revising and Proofreading

Directions: Choose the <u>one best answer</u> to each question.

Questions 1–10 refer to the following instructions.

(1) Hiking is fun, but you has to use common sense. (2) Never throw or roll rocks; there may be hikers below. (3) These narrow canyons are especially dangerous. (4) Walking through the park, narrow canyons can be seen. (5) Broked rocks often fall from the cliffs into these canyons. (6) Whether hiking driving or climbing your safety depends on your good judgment. (7) Dont ruin your vacation by having an accident. (8) The dessert is dry, even in winter. (9) Water is available at the visitors' center. (10) Carry enough water for everyone in your group.

1. Sentence 1: **Hiking is fun, but you has to use common sense**.

    Which correction should be made to sentence 1?

    (1) To hike is fun, but you has to use common sense.

    (2) Hiking are fun, but you has to use common sense.

    (3) Hiking is fun, but you have to use common sense.

    (4) Hiking is fun, but you are having to use common sense.

    (5) Hiking are fun, but you have to use common sense.

2. Sentence 2: **Never throw or roll rocks; there may be hikers below.**

    Which is the best way to write this sentence?

    (1) No change

    (2) Never throw or roll rocks there may be hikers below.

    (3) Never throw or roll rocks, there may be hikers below.

    (4) Never throw or roll rocks yet there may be hikers below.

    (5) Never throw or roll rocks so there may be hikers below.

3. Sentence 3: **These narrow canyons are especially dangerous**.

   Which revisions should be made to the placement of sentence 3?

   (1) Place it first in the paragraph.

   (2) Place it after sentence 1.

   (3) Switch the order of sentences 3 and 4.

   (4) Place it after sentence 5.

   (5) Place it after sentence 6.

4. Sentence 4: **Walking through the park, narrow canyons can be seen.**

   Which correction should be made to sentence 4?

   (1) Walking through the park, narrow canyons can be seen by you.

   (2) As you walk through the park, you can see narrow canyons.

   (3) As they walk through the park, narrow canyons can be seen.

   (4) Narrow canyons can be seen walking through the park.

   (5) Narrow canyons, walking through the park, can be seen.

5. Sentence 5: **<u>Broked</u> rocks often fall from the cliffs into these canyons.**

   Which is the best way to rewrite the underlined portion of this sentence?

   (1) No change

   (2) Broke

   (3) Broken

   (4) Breaks

   (5) Having breaked

6. Sentence 6: **<u>Whether hiking driving or climbing your</u> safety depends on your good judgment.**

   Which is the best way to rewrite the underlined portion of this sentence?

   (1) No change

   (2) Whether hiking driving, or climbing your

   (3) Whether, hiking, driving, or, climbing your

   (4) Whether hiking driving or, climbing your

   (5) Whether hiking, driving, or climbing, your

7. Sentence 7: **<u>Dont</u> ruin your vacation by having an accident.**

   Which is the best way to rewrite the underlined portion of this sentence?

   (1) No change

   (2) Don't

   (3) Don't'

   (4) Dont'

   (5) Do'nt

8. Sentence 8: **The dessert is dry, even in winter.**

Which correction should be made to sentence 4?

(1) Change <u>is</u> to <u>are</u>

(2) Change <u>dry</u> to <u>drie</u>

(3) Change <u>dessert</u> to <u>desert</u>

(4) Change <u>dessert</u> to <u>desserrt</u>

(5) Change <u>dessert</u> to <u>deserrt</u>

9. Sentences 9 and 10: **Water is available at the visitors' center. Carry enough water for everyone in your group**

Which is the best way to combine these sentences?

(1) So carry enough water for everyone in your group, water is available at the visitors' center.

(2) Carry enough water for everyone in your group, because water is available at the visitors' center.

(3) Water is available at the visitors' center, since you carry enough water for everyone in your group.

(4) Even though water is available at the visitors' center, carry enough water for everyone in your group.

(5) Water is available at the visitors' center, carry enough water for everyone in your group.

10. Which sentence best concludes this passage?

(1) Do not drink untreated water.

(2) Use these suggestions and common sense to have a safe time in the park.

(3) Stay on the trail when you hike.

(4) Be sure to obey warnings that you will see posted on trees.

(5) Parents: watch your children!

Essay

Directions: At the end of this book or on separate sheets of paper, write the following essay. Be sure to revise and proofread your essay. Use the Essay Evaluation Guide at the end of this posttest after you've written your essay.

Suppose you won a million dollars. In your essay, tell what you would do with the money and explain your reasons for using it this way. Use your personal observations, experience, and knowledge to support your ideas.

Answers to Organization

1. **The correct answer is (2).** This sentence gives a broad overview of the topic of the letter: the excellent staff at the public library. The other choices provide details or are not on the topic. Review Chapter 1 for more information on topic sentences.

2. **The correct answer is (1).** Since sentence 3 provides details about sentence 1, it should follow directly after it. See Chapter 2 to review unity and coherence in writing.

3. **The correct answer is (2).** The transition "Second" most logically follows "First of all" and serves to introduce the second main point the writing is making. See Chapter 2 for a review of unity and coherence in writing.

4. **The correct answer is (4).** Herman's interest in TV over books has nothing to do with the library staff's excellent service. See Chapter 2 for a review of unity and coherence in writing.

5. **The correct answer is (1).** This sentence best sums up the writer's main point: the Springdale Public Library has a superb staff. See Chapter 2 for a review of unity and coherence in writing.

Answers to Sentence Structure

1. **The correct answer is (3).** As written, the sentence is a run-on, two complete sentences run together without correct punctuation. Only choice (3) correctly joins the two sentences. Review Chapter 4 for more information on run-ons.

2. **The correct answer is (5).** As written, the sentence is a fragment, an incomplete sentence. This sentence is missing a verb. Only choice (5) correctly supplies the missing verb. Review Chapter 4 for more information on fragments.

3. **The correct answer is (5).** As written, this is a dangling modifier—a word or phrase that describes something that has been left out of the sentence. Only choice (5) provides the missing noun. Review Chapter 5 for more information on dangling and misplaced modifiers.

4. **The correct answer is (2).** As written, this is a misplaced modifier—a word or phrase placed too far from the noun it describes. Only choice (2) places the modifier ("with a problem") in its correct place after "customers." Review Chapter 5 for more information on dangling and misplaced modifiers.

5. **The correct answer is (2).** *Parallel words* share the same part of speech. They can all be nouns, adjectives, or verbs, for example. The words must also be in the same tense (if they are verbs). This means they must all be in the past, present, or future. As written, the sentence is not parallel. Only choice (2) corrects the error in parallelism by matching "check in," " take a number," and "wait in line." Review Chapter 6 for more information on parallel structure.

Answers to Usage

1. **The correct answer is (5).** The plural subject <u>Dr. Roberts and Ms. Harris</u> requires the plural verb <u>have</u>. See Chapter 7 for more information on subject-verb agreement.

2. **The correct answer is (3).** The plural subject <u>All employees</u> requires the plural verb <u>are</u>. See Chapter 7 for more information on subject-verb agreement.

3. **The correct answer is (2).** *You* is always used with the base form of the verb. The base form of *learn* is "learn." See Chapter 7 for more information on subject-verb agreement.

4. **The correct answer is (2).** *Irregular verbs* don't form the past by adding *-ed* or *-d*. The past tense and past participle are formed in many different ways. The past participle of *give* is "given." See Chapter 8 for more information on verbs.

5. **The correct answer is (4).** A verb is *passive* when its action is performed upon the subject, as shown in the original sentence. In general, use the active voice instead of the passive voice. The active voice is less wordy and more direct than the passive voice. Only choice (4) is the active voice. See Chapter 8 for more information on active and passive voice.

Answers to Mechanics

1. **The correct answer is (5).** Capitalize the first word of a sentence and months. Use a comma after an opening phrase or clause. See Chapters 9 and 10 for more information on capitalization and punctuation.

2. **The correct answer is (2).** Form contractions correctly. See Chapter 11 to review contractions.

3. **The correct answer is (3).** Capitalize a person's name. See Chapter 9 to review capitalization.

4. **The correct answer is (4).** Use a semicolon between main clauses when the coordinating conjunction has been left out. See Chapter 10 to review punctuation.

5. **The correct answer is (2).** With singular nouns, add an apostrophe and an *s* to the word doing the owning. Here, the bank is doing the owning of its officers; they are the "officers of the bank." Neither "officers" nor "customers" shows ownership; rather, both are merely plural. See Chapter 11 to review possessives.

Answers to the Writing Test

The following model essay would earn a very high score on the GED Language Arts, Writing Test. Compare it to your own essay to assess your strengths and weaknesses.

Most people are quick to condemn television as bad for children, but I think TV has a lot going for it. In fact, television has helped me in three very important ways. First, watching television helped me learn English. Second, it taught me a lot about American culture. Finally, television helped me stay out of trouble when I was younger. Television was especially important to me when I first came to America.

When I came to the United States, I spoke only a few words of English, but television came to my rescue. Because I was twelve years old, I was placed in the seventh grade. I was the same age as every other student in the classroom, but I could not talk with a single person. When I got home from school every day, I watched cartoons and the news. As I learned more English, I started watching comedy shows and soap operas. My English got better fast. As a result, I was able to talk more easily with my classmates and teacher and so did much better in school. I made some friends, too, and felt more at home in my new country. By helping me learn English, television helped me fit into American life.

Television also helped me learn about American culture. I found out from watching television that life in America is different from life in my birthplace, Korea. In Korea, for example, most of the television commercials are about education. In America, however, most of the commercials are about cars, food, and clothing. This suggested to me that Americans are encouraged to buy things. Watching TV helped me realize what American life is like much more quickly.

Finally, watching television helped me stay out of trouble. I saw commercials about drug and alcohol abuse. These commercials helped me realize the importance of staying straight. Also, I did not go out at night because I preferred to be inside watching my favorite shows, especially movies.

As an immigrant, I found television a good way to learn English. TV also helped me learn about American culture. Television also encouraged me avoid drug and alcohol abuse and even gangs. TV helped me a lot.

Answers to Revising and Proofreading

1. **The correct answer is (3).** *Agreement* is matching subject and verb. When subjects and verbs agree, your sentences sound smooth and correct. With the pronoun *you,* the correct form of the verb "to be" is "have." See Chapter 7 to review agreement.

2. **The correct answer is (1).** Use a semicolon to connect two closely related independent clauses (two complete sentences). See Chapters 3 and 4 to review sentence structure.

3. **The correct answer is (3).** This sentence should follow the next one, not come before it. See Chapter 2 to review unity and coherence.

4. **The correct answer is (2).** As written, the sentence is a dangling modifier—a word or phrase that describes something that has been left out of the sentence. Only choice (2) corrects the error by providing a noun or pronoun to which the dangling modifier can be linked. See Chapter 5 for a review of dangling and misplaced modifiers.

5. **The correct answer is (3).** The correct past participle of "break" is "broken," the meaning required by the sentence. See Chapter 8 to review verb usage.

6. **The correct answer is (5).** Use a comma to separate items in a series. Also use a comma before an opening group of words. See Chapter 10 to review comma use.

7. **The correct answer is (2).** Use an apostrophe (') in a contraction where one or more letters have been left out. Here, the phrase is *do not*, so the contraction is *don't*. See Chapter 11 to review how to spell contractions.

8. **The correct answer is (3).** The word "desert" refers to the arid wasteland; "dessert" is the sweet at the end of a meal. See Chapter 11 to review how to spell confusing words.

9. **The correct answer is (4).** When you subordinate one part of a sentence, you make the dependent clause develop the independent clause. Make the first clause—"Water is available at the visitors' center"—the dependent clause. Make the second clause—"Carry enough water for everyone in your group"—the main clause. Use the subordinating conjunction *even though* to join the two clauses. This creates a logical linking of ideas. See Chapters 3 and 4 to review sentence structure.

10. **The correct answer is (2).** Choice (2) restates the topic sentence and the main ideas in this paragraph. The other choices are details, not a restatement of the main idea. See Chapters 1 and 2 to review unity and coherence.

Essay Evaluation Guide

Use this checklist as you assess your essays.

1. **Main Ideas**

   _____ Do my main points directly answer the question?

   _____ Are my main points persuasive and logical? Will they convince my readers that my point is valid?

   _____ Are my ideas linked in a logical way? Does my essay have unity?

2. **Organization**

   _____ Does my essay have a clear beginning that introduces my main points?

   _____ Does my essay have at least two body paragraphs? Do I start a new paragraph for each main point?

   _____ Does my essay have a conclusion that sums up my main points?

3. **Development of ideas**

   _____ Do I include specific details to make my point? (*Details* are examples, facts, statistics, reasons, definitions, and descriptions.)

   _____ Are my facts correct?

   _____ Do my details really prove my point?

4. **Skills**

   _____ Have I spelled all words correctly?

   _____ Have I used correct grammar?

   _____ Have I corrected all errors in punctuation and capitalization?

   _____ Can my handwriting be read easily? Have I written in pen?

Appendices

Appendices

Sample Essays A

Obviously, there's no single correct way to write any of the essays in this appendix.

These essays are meant only as rough guides and examples of how an essay question could be approached. Your essay can look very different from ours and still be a high-scoring essay. However, if you're having problems approaching a particular question, sometimes it can be helpful to see how someone else wrote on that same topic. Please note that the opinions expressed in these essays do not reflect the view of the publisher, editor, or author of this book—they are just examples to show how a student could answer a question if he or she chose.

Sample Essay 1

Write an essay in which you examine how art has had an impact on your life or on the life of someone else.

I feel strongly that art can have a direct influence on people's lives. It may be as small as brightening someone's day or causing someone to think about a topic they had never explored before. However, sometimes art's effect can be much greater. In the following essay I'll explain one way in which art changed the life of one of my family members.

When my uncle was in the hospital with intestinal problems, he was in extreme pain. My aunt brought him a painting that he had in his office at home because she knew he loved it. It wasn't a famous painting, but one his father painted when he was young, and it really expressed my uncle's father's joyful spirit.

The whole three weeks my uncle was in the hospital, he would spend hours each day just looking at that painting. One of the nurses commented that he had been using a lot more pain medication before my aunt brought the painting. My uncle really felt that having the painting there and looking at it instead of the boring hospital walls brought him relief from pain and helped him heal more quickly than he would have otherwise.

Of course, there's no way to know for sure if the painting did have any effect on his pain tolerance or healing rate. What matters is that he thought it did, so he felt better when the painting was there for him to look at. He's been out of the hospital for two years now, and he still makes sure to look at the painting (which is back on the wall in his home office) at least once a day. He credits that painting with restoring his vitality when he was extremely weak, and maybe even saving his life.

In conclusion, I don't think my uncle's story is at all unusual. Healing from illness because of beautiful art or music or literature is probably an "everyday miracle," and may be at least as common as near-death experiences are. But that doesn't mean that its impact on my uncle's life wasn't significant. Because of that, I believe strongly in the healing power of art.

Sample Essay 2

In attempting to make a decision, some people try to compromise, while others try to enforce their own opinions. Write an essay in which you examine how this choice affects the people involved in the decision.

When groups of people try to make a decision, they need to know whether the decision will be made on the basis of consensus, majority rule, or absolute power. People usually base their actions around the way in which the decision will be made. For instance, a shy person will probably be more comfortable speaking up in a process in which the group must reach consensus than in one in which one person gets to overrule everyone else. A person who knows that she is good at persuading other people to do what she wants doesn't have any reason to join a group that uses consensus. This means that people who choose the groups they belong to are usually satisfied with the process of decision-making, even if they're not that happy about the actual result.

Sometimes, however, people don't have any idea how a group makes decisions. This is when feelings get hurt and people get angry. This probably happens most often when people try to force their own opinions upon others. In the process of trying to argue their own opinions, many times people sink to accusing other people of having "wrong" opinions or even insult them personally. So what should have been a calm, rational discussion becomes an all-out fight. The losers of the process end up feeling hurt, used, and resentful. Even the winner can feel tired and resentful, if not ashamed.

Even though consensus seems to be a better way to make decisions without hurting anyone's feelings, this method of decision-making has problems, too. The group has to discuss the situation over and over again until everyone agrees, so the process can go on for hours or days. And if people really disagree, getting everyone to agree can be extremely difficult. By the time the process is over, everyone in the group can feel exhausted and annoyed with each other. This may make them not want to come together again to make another decision.

On the other hand, sometimes people become much closer after having gone through a difficult decision-making process through consensus. Last year, our cheerleading squad had to decide whether we needed new uniforms or not. If we got new uniforms, we thought we would look better at state championships. But getting new uniforms meant doing fundraisers to raise the money to buy them, and some people thought it would be too much work to add to our practice schedule and schoolwork. It took us three whole practices to decide, and a couple of times, some people started yelling. But once we decided to get the new uniforms, we all felt closer than ever. I hope we don't have to make another decision like that anytime soon, but our team is definitely stronger because we used consensus.

The process one uses to make decisions can strongly affect the way people feel about each other and about the decision. There is no one way to decide that guarantees that no one will feel bad, however. The people involved in the process just have to stay as calm as possible and try to see it from the other person's point of view. Then they will be able to come together without fighting.

Sample Essay 3

Write an essay in which you examine how your family dynamics affect the way you approach friendships.

I believe the dynamics in my family have affected the way I approach friendships very strongly. I am the middle child of five; I have two older brothers and two younger sisters. My brothers are always rough-housing and horsing around, and many times they include me. They seldom play with my sisters, however, because they are much younger than I am. Because of my relationship with my brothers, I think I look for friends who are very dynamic and athletic, because I look up to my brothers very much. I guess I'm really hoping to find friends who are just like my brothers but are my age.

I also feel a special bond with my little sisters, because we three women have to stick together. As they get older, I want to tell them all about how life works, how to deal with boys, and how to use makeup. I take my role as an older sister very seriously, and I have a lot of friends who also have younger siblings and want to be a good example for them.

My relationship with my parents is also very important to me because I have worked hard to earn their trust. My parents are very strict, but I appreciate that; they have to be strict because they have five children. Without a strong sense of order in a household of seven different people, life might become very disorganized. Therefore, I am not inclined to be friends with people who just wait around until their parents go out of town so they can have a big party and go crazy. Acting out like that is really just a lame cry for attention, and all it does is show disrespect for the parents that raised you.

Therefore, I conclude that I have found a lot of friends who for the most part think the way that I do regarding the importance of family. I am lucky that I have older brothers to look up to, younger sisters to be a role model for, and parents who trust me to do the right thing. As a result, I feel the dynamics in my family have helped me find friends who feel the same way.

Sample Essay 4

Write a letter to the head of your local school board arguing that the school day should start and end 45 minutes later.

Dear Sir:

I am writing to ask you to consider altering the state-mandated school-day schedule by making the school day start and end 45 minutes later. I think students would benefit from the extra sleep in the morning, and I believe the time shift would allow students to devote more time to learning and studying in the middle of the day, when they are at their best.

Teenaged people need a lot more rest than most of us get on a nightly basis. Studies show that the average person aged 13–18 needs nine to ten hours of sleep per night in order to maintain the best health. Unfortunately, most high school students are so consumed by studies and extracurricular activities (not to mention the stress of measuring up to the standards set by our parents); we average only four to six hours of sleep per night.

Starting school at 9:00 rather than 8:15 would give the average student the chance to rest after busy days of school, homework, and whatever other activities we are involved in, and arrive ready to learn and feeling more refreshed. I know I am not a morning person, and a number of my friends are not as well, because we stay up late into the night studying. We would all benefit from an extra hour of sleep.

As far as the end of the school day is concerned, keeping kids a little longer in the afternoon can also be beneficial. With less emphasis on the early morning, students can concentrate better. There are also smaller children who have single or working parents and need to be kept active (but supervised) until their parents can come and collect them.

In conclusion, I sincerely feel that it is in the best interest of students to start and end the school day later than the current schedule dictates. It would help students concentrate better, it would keep kids occupied longer into the afternoon, and it would have no effect on the length of the school day, which is harder to change.

I hope that you will consider my opinion and make this important change that could help so many teenaged people.

Sincerely,

Jin Yoo

Sample Essay 5

Write a letter to your city council requesting that fines be doubled for parking in disabled parking spaces without a permit.

To the Llanview City Council:

I am writing this letter to request that you raise the fine for parking in a disabled parking space without a disabled parking sticker from $180 to $360. I realize that to double the fine may seem outrageous to some members of our community, but it is practically nothing when you consider how serious the crime is. Please allow me to explain why I think this crime is so horrible.

Disabled people really need these parking spaces close to stores and offices. Most people immediately think of a person in a wheelchair when they think of a disabled person and wonder what the big deal is to just roll a chair a few more yards. But the reality is that many people with disabilities don't use wheelchairs but may have trouble walking. They may have problems with their legs, breathing problems, tremors, or any number of other disabilities. If they can't be guaranteed a parking space very close to a building, they will not be able to make it from their cars to the building.

If they do not make it from their cars to the building, this means they will have to stay home. If they stay home, they will not be able to get the things they need to survive, like food and clothing, not to mention the things that make life nicer, like books or videos or art supplies. If they want these things, they will have to figure out a way to get them delivered, which usually costs extra. This is a big problem, since most disabled people already live on fixed incomes or incomes that are less than the ones that the general population has. So, in essence, by not having disabled parking spaces, we are reducing the incomes of disabled people even more.

This means that whenever someone who is not disabled parks in a disabled parking space, the able-bodied person is stealing directly from disabled people and restricting their lives. I'm sure that you would be furious if someone didn't let you go to the store. That's how disabled people must feel whenever they try to park and find someone in their space who shouldn't be there.

In conclusion, I feel that because parking in a disabled parking space without a disabled sticker is a crime that directly hurts people, the fine should be much greater than $180 and should be raised to $360. Maybe this would make law-breakers think twice about parking in places they shouldn't. By walking a few extra yards they could save themselves a lot of money and make life easier for someone who needs it. Please consider my proposal and raise the fee.

Sincerely,

Travis Stone

Sample Essay 6

Write a letter to your community college requesting to enter the journalism program as a sophomore instead of a freshman.

To Whom It May Concern:

I am writing to request that you allow me to enter the journalism program at Monroe County Community College (MCCC) as a sophomore, not a freshman. I have excellent test scores, four years of journalism experience, and extra credits that should be applied to my record.

I have excellent test scores, which are above the average for the journalism program at MCCC. I scored a 580 on the verbal part of the SAT, which is above the MCCC average of 490 and the journalism program's average of 550. This reflects my strong vocabulary and command of the English language. I have never gotten any grade lower than an A– in any of my English classes. I also scored well on the ACT.

I wrote for my high school paper for three years. I also write articles for our neighborhood weekly newspaper. The other reporters for this paper are adults with college degrees, so I am doing the job of a professional journalist.

I also have six extra college-level credits. I earned these the last two summers by going to a special journalism camp at Denison University. I am enclosing a copy of the transcripts from this program. You will see that I got As in all the courses I took there.

Please allow me to enter the MCCC journalism program this fall as a sophomore. I am qualified and will work hard to make sure I pass my classes with flying colors.

Sincerely,

Katie Watson

Sample Essay 7

Do you think that the minimum wage should be raised? Explain your opinion.

Some people think that the minimum wage should not be raised because this would hurt free enterprise. I strongly disagree with this statement; I believe the minimum wage should be raised.

The current minimum wage is extremely low. A single person could barely live on it, let alone a family of two or more. The only way a person here in Milwaukee could survive on minimum wage would be working 60 hours a week every week. This means that when other people are at home with their families or in their beds, a minimum wage earner is still working. This is not fair.

Raising the minimum wage would allow people to work shorter hours and still be able to rent an apartment and pay for food and clothes. This is a basic right of all humans, and we have a duty to make it possible for people to feed their families without going on government assistance.

There are people who believe that raising the minimum wage would hurt businesses, but it would actually help businesses in the long run. If the minimum wage were raised, workers would have more money to spend. They would spend this money, and it would go back to the companies. Thus, the companies would make more profits in the long run.

In short, we need to raise the minimum wage because we need to start treating people fairly. The fact that doing this would also help businesses is a nice bonus.

Sample Essay 8

Write a letter to the director of an amusement park requesting an interview for a job for the summer.

Dear Employment Director,

I am writing to request an interview for a job working at Great Adventure this summer. I have been going to Great Adventure since I was 10, and I love it. Nothing would make me happier than to work at the park this summer.

I have experience in food service from working at my dad's pizza store. I have been cleaning there for the past four years and working the counter for the past year. My skills are speed, accuracy with the orders, and making change in my head.

I would also love to work on one of the roller coasters. My favorite is the Twisting Dragon because it is the highest, scariest coaster in the park. I have always wanted to be one of the people who make sure that everyone is belted in safely before the ride starts. I've even been practicing giving the thumbs-up sign.

While food service and roller coasters are my two main areas of interest, I would love to do any job at Great Adventure. I hope that you will contact me about an interview soon. You may call me at home at 609-555-1111. Thank you for your time.

Sincerely,

Joshua Banks

Sample Essay 9

Write a letter to a camera manufacturer asking for a replacement for the camera that broke the first day you used it.

To Whom It May Concern:

I am writing to you to ask for a replacement camera for your model XV-500. I bought this camera on March 3, and it broke when I used it for the first time on March 4. I read the instruction book thoroughly before I even put the battery in the camera to make sure I could operate it properly. However, when I pressed the button to pull back the lens cap, the lens cap broke. I took the camera back to the store that I bought it from, but they told me to contact you directly to get a replacement.

My mother bought the same camera as a gift for my grandmother last Christmas, and she has been very happy with it. So I was very surprised when mine broke before I could even take one picture with it. I hope that you will send me a new camera soon so that I can begin taking pictures.

Sincerely,

Marc Garcia

Sample Essay 10

Which is more important: duty to yourself or duty to others?

It is extremely difficult to answer the question of whether duty to yourself or duty to others is more important.

On the one hand, duty to yourself could be seen as being the most important thing of all. After all, if you don't look out for yourself, you can't expect anyone else to either. And once you fulfill your duty to yourself, you are free to help others without worrying that you are shortchanging yourself by putting others first. An example of this would be on an airplane. If the pressure changes and the oxygen masks drop down, you are supposed to put your own on first before you help anyone else. This is a metaphor for the rest of life, in that you can't help others if you haven't taken care of your own needs first.

On the other hand, duty to yourself could be seen as a selfish choice when others are in need of help. After all, if everyone neglected the needs of other people in favor of their own, there would be little human communication in the world, and the problems that we have already would grow bigger and bigger. However, if everyone fulfilled their duty to help others, we would all get exactly what we need from other people. There would be no need to focus on ourselves, since other people would be helping us, and we would be helping them.

Realistically, however, there will always be people who won't do their duty to others. Unfortunately, there are always selfish people who don't look out for others. This is especially horrible when they act selfishly but don't even do things that are for their own good. For example, some people think that they have the right to smoke wherever they want to. This is not doing their duty to others because it exposes others to secondhand smoke and also annoys them. But it also isn't duty to self, since smoking will eventually kill you in a gruesome and painful way.

In conclusion, it would be nice if people would dedicate themselves to helping others. But this will never happen, so the best we can hope for is that people truly take themselves seriously and do what is right for themselves. Maybe then they will have some energy left over to help others, even if it isn't their first priority.

Sample Essay 11

Which statement has more value: "Never judge a book by its cover" or "The first impression is the lasting impression"?

This is an interesting question, because it reminds me of another two proverbs that contradict each other: "He who hesitates is lost" and "Look before you leap." Both have merit, but they can't both be correct. In the case of this topic, however, I believe the first statement has more value than the second, because one is a response to the other; people are usually very judgmental, and they should be reminded not to be.

It is true that "a first impression is a lasting impression." When I moved to my new school three years ago, I was very hopeful that the students would like me, but I had no idea how to act. I did my best to act cool, but on my third day, I tripped in the lunchroom and dropped my lunch tray, spilling soup all over the floor. To this day, even though I have known my friends for years now, they still call me "Soupy."

I realize I am fortunate that I can look back on the incident and laugh. The other students could have easily dismissed me as some sort of geek and not accept me. But the people who became my friends saw beyond the first impression I made and got to know me as a person. Still, that first impression has stayed with me, and I bet these guys will call me "Soupy" until I'm 90 years old.

So, in conclusion, both of these sayings are very commonly heard in modern society, and though they seem to say opposite things, they are actually related. A first impression does make a lasting impression, but that isn't the way it should be. So, if you ever find yourself in the position to judge someone based on a first impression that might not be indicative of that person as a whole, you should remember not to judge a book by its cover.

Sample Essay 12

Have computers improved the quality of life? Why or why not?

Much has been said about how computers make our lives easier. With the click of a mouse, we can pay bills, shop, chat with others, or find the latest news or sports scores. It's true that computers have made finding information a lot easier, but the price of this convenience is a lot higher than people think.

Firstly, I believe computers are removing the human element for our society. Chat rooms are replacing discussions, ATMs are taking over for bank tellers, and online shopping is replacing visits to the store. All of this might appear more convenient, but the downside is that we're becoming lazier and less accustomed to face-to-face contact. If the current pattern continues, there might not be any reason to leave the house in fifty years.

Secondly, computers have made it easier for corporations to spy on us and get an idea of our interests so that they can send us piles of spam e-mails. Some sites, for example, have software that keeps track of our previous purchases and offers recommendations to buy more items that we don't want or need. This type of invasion of privacy makes me think of George Orwell's novel, 1984.

Thirdly, since just about everything is now run by a computer, it is scary to think about what could happen if they break down. I remember how concerned everyone was about the Y2K bug a few years ago, and how it could affect power plants, medical equipment, air traffic control devices, and all sorts of other things that need to function properly all the time. Computers have become so common, we don't even realize what kind of chaos could happen as the result of vandalism or a major malfunction.

I think I am in the minority on this topic, because most people really like computers. But, in my opinion, computers have made us more content to avoid human contact, more susceptible to corporate greed, and more vulnerable to a complete shutdown of important services. Since computers are here to stay, however, it's important for people like me to learn to live with them.

Essay Evaluation Guide B

Use this checklist as you assess your essays.

1. **Main Ideas**

_____ Do my main points directly answer the question?

_____ Are my main points persuasive and logical? Will they convince my readers that my point is valid?

_____ Are my ideas linked in a logical way? Does my essay have unity?

2. **Organization**

_____ Does my essay have a clear beginning that introduces my main points?

_____ Does my essay have at least two body paragraphs? Do I start a new paragraph for each main point?

_____ Does my essay have a conclusion that sums up my main points?

3. **Development of ideas**

_____ Do I include specific details to make my point? (*Details* are examples, facts, statistics, reasons, definitions, and descriptions.)

_____ Are my facts correct?

_____ Do my details really prove my point?

4. **Skills**

_____ Have I spelled all words correctly?

_____ Have I used correct grammar?

_____ Have I corrected all errors in punctuation and capitalization?

_____ Can my handwriting be read easily? Have I written in pen?

About the GED | C

What to Expect on the GED

There are five GED tests:

- Language Arts, Writing
- Mathematics
- Science
- Social Studies
- Language Arts, Reading

With the exception of the Language Arts, Writing Test, all GED tests are in multiple-choice format. Each multiple-choice question will have five possible answer choices, and you must choose the best answer for each question. The multiple-choice questions may be based on a graphic, a text, or a mathematics problem, or they might just test your knowledge of a particular subject. Let's take a look at the kinds of questions asked on each subject area test:

Language Arts, Writing

The multiple-choice section of the Language Arts, Writing Test examines your knowledge of English grammar and usage. It contains several passages and accompanying questions that ask you to find errors or determine the best way to rewrite particular sentences from the passage. The essay section requires you to write a 200- to 250-word essay on a particular topic in 45 minutes. This question won't test your knowledge of a particular subject, such as the War of 1812 or the Pythagorean theorem. Instead, you are asked to write about your own life experiences. The readers of the essay will not be grading the essay based on how much you know or don't know about the topic but rather on how well you use standard English.

Social Studies

The Social Studies Test contains multiple-choice questions on history, economics, political science, and geography. In the United States, the test focuses on U.S. history and government, while the test in Canada focuses on Canadian history and government. World history is included, too. Some of the questions will be based on reading passages, and some questions will be based on graphics such as maps, charts, illustrations, or political cartoons.

Science

The Science Test contains multiple-choice questions on physical and life sciences. You will also see questions on earth science, space science, life science, health science, and environmental science. As with the Social Studies Test, some of the science questions will be based on reading passages, and others will be based on graphics such as scientific diagrams.

Language Arts, Reading

The Language Arts, Reading Test is similar to the Social Studies and Science Tests in that the multiple-choice questions will be based on passages. The passages in this test are longer than the passages in the other subject area tests. In the Language Arts, Reading Test, some of the questions will be based on poems, some on prose, some on pieces of drama, and some on documents that you might encounter in the workplace.

Mathematics

There are two parts to the Mathematics Test. You can use a calculator on Part I, but not on Part II. The Mathematics Test uses multiple-choice questions to measure your skills in arithmetic, algebra, geometry, and problem solving. Some of the questions will ask you to find the answer to a problem, while others will require you to find the best way to solve the problem. Many of the questions will be based on diagrams. Some of the questions will be grouped into sets that require you to draw upon information from a number of sources, such as graphs and charts.

The majority of GED questions on all five of the tests measure your skills and test-taking abilities. What does this mean for you? This means that if you work hard to sharpen your test-taking skills, you will be much more prepared for success on the tests than if you sat down and memorized names, dates, facts, properties, charts, or other bits of information. Basically, you will have more success on the GED if you know how to take the tests than if all you know is information about reading, writing, science, social studies, and math. Let's look at some strategies for answering multiple-choice questions.

Answering Multiple-Choice Questions

The key to success on multiple-choice tests is understanding the questions and how to find the correct answer. Each multiple-choice question on the GED will be followed by five answer choices: (1), (2), (3), (4), and (5). There will be no trick questions and no questions intended to confuse you. If you use the strategies that follow, you will be very successful on the multiple-choice questions.

Strategies for Attacking Multiple-Choice Questions

- **Read the question carefully and make sure you know what it is asking.** Read each question slowly. If you rush through the question, you might miss a key word that could cost you the correct answer. You might want to run your pencil under the question as you read it to be sure that you don't miss anything in the question. If you don't understand the question after the first time you read it, go back and read it another time or two until you understand it.

- **Don't overanalyze the question.** Many test-takers make the mistake of overanalyzing questions, looking for some trick or hidden meaning that the test-creators added for the sake of confusion. The GED creators don't do that on any of the questions, so take each question at face value. Each question will say exactly what it means, so don't try to interpret something unusual into the questions.

- **Circle or underline the key words in the question.** As you read through the question, locate any important words in the question and either circle or underline the word or words. Important words will be anything taken directly from the chart, table, graph, or reading passage on which the question is based. Other important words will be words like *compare, contrast, similar, different,* or *main idea.* By circling or underlining the key words, you will understand the question better and will be more prepared to recognize the correct answer.

- **After you read the question, try to answer it in your head before you look at the answer choices.** If you think you know the answer to the question without even looking at the answer choices, then you most likely will recognize the correct answer right away when you read the possible answer choices. Also, if you think you know the correct answer right away, then you should be very confident in your answer when you find it listed among the possible answer choices.

- **Try covering the answer choices while you are reading the question.** To try answering the question in your head without being influenced by the answer choices, cover the answer choices with your hand as you read the question. This technique will also help prevent you from reading something into the question that isn't there based on something you saw in one of the answer choices. Covering the answer choices may also help you concentrate only on the question to make sure you read it carefully and correctly.

- **Carefully read all the answer choices before answering the question.** You need to look at all the possibilities before you choose the best answer. Even if you think you know the answer before looking at the possible answer choices, read all of the answer choices anyway. If you read through two of the answer choices and you find that choice (3) is a good answer, keep reading because choice (4) or (5) may be a better answer. Finally, by reading all the answer choices, you can be more confident in your answer because you will see that the others are definitely incorrect.

- **Eliminate answer choices that you know are wrong.** As you read through all the choices, some will obviously be incorrect. When you find those answer choices, mark them as incorrect. This will help you narrow the possible choices. In addition, crossing out incorrect answers will prevent you from choosing an incorrect answer by mistake.

- **Don't spend too much time on one question.** If you read a question and you just can't seem to find the best or correct answer, circle the question, skip it, and come back to it later. Your time will be better spent answering questions that you can answer. Your time is limited, so don't struggle with one question if you could correctly answer three others in the same amount of time.

- **Go with your first answer.** Once you choose an answer, stick to it. A test-taker's first hunch is usually the correct one. There is a reason why your brain told you to choose a particular answer, so stand by it. Also, don't waste time debating over whether the answer you chose is correct. Go with your first answer and move on.

- **Don't go back and change your answer unless you have a good, solid reason to do so.** Remember that your first hunch is usually the best, so don't change your answer on a whim. One of the only times you should change your answer on a previous question is if you find something later in the test that contradicts what you chose. The only other time you should change an answer is if you remember very clearly a teacher's lecture, a reading passage, or some other reliable source of information to the contrary of what you chose.

- **Look for hints within the answer choices.** For example, some sets of answer choices may contain two choices that vary by only a word or two. Chances are that the correct answer is one of those two answers.

- **Watch out for absolutes.** Other hints within answer choices can be words called absolutes. These words include *always, never, only,* or *completely*. These words severely limit the possibility of that answer choice being right.

- **If you just don't know the correct answer, guess.** That's right, guess. The GED Tests are scored based on how many questions you answer correctly, and there is no point penalty for answering incorrectly. Therefore, why leave questions unanswered? If you do, you have no chance at getting any points for those. However, if you guess, you at least have a chance to get some points. Before you guess, try to eliminate as many wrong answer choices as possible. You have a much greater chance of choosing the correct answer if you can weed out some that are incorrect. This strategy is especially helpful if you have several questions left for which you are going to guess.

- **Be aware of how much time you have left on the test.** However, don't glance down at your watch or up at the clock after every question to check the time. Occasional glimpses at the clock should be sufficient to monitor your time. You will be instructed at the beginning of the test as to the amount of time you have to complete the test. Just be aware of that amount of time. The creators of the GED Tests designed the tests and test times so that you will have ample time to complete the tests. As you approach the point at which you have 10 minutes left, make sure that you are not spending your time answering the difficult questions if you still have other questions ahead of you that you can answer. If you have answered all the questions that you can with relatively little difficulty, go back and work on those that gave you trouble. If you come down to the wire and have a few left, guess at the answers. There is no penalty for wrong answers on the GED.

- **If you have time left at the end of the test, go back to any questions that you skipped.** As you just read, after you finish all the questions that you can without too much difficulty, you should go back over the test and find the ones you skipped. The amount of time you have left should determine the amount of time you spend on each unanswered question. For example, if you have 10 questions left and 10 minutes left, try to work on a few of them. However, if you have 10 questions left and 2 minutes left, go through and guess on each of the remaining questions.

What's Next?

Working with this book is the first step toward getting your GED. But what should you do next? Many people find it helpful to take a GED test-preparation course. Call your local high school counselor or the Adult Education or Continuing Education Department at your local community college, college, or university. The people in those offices can tell you where courses are offered and how to enroll. In addition to taking a GED course, continue studying on your own with this book and others in the ARCO line of books.

Once you feel ready to take the tests, contact the GED Testing Service to find out when and where the exams will be administered next:

General Educational Development
GED Testing Service
American Council on Education
One Dupont Circle, NW
Washington, DC 20036

Phone: 800-626-9433 (toll-free)

Web site: www.gedtest.org

Good luck!

Use the Following Pages for Your Essays

Practice makes perfect!

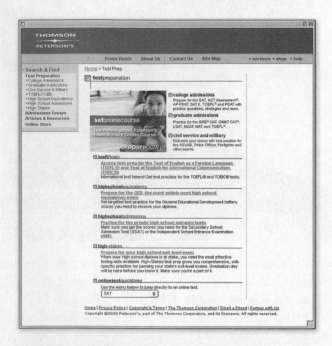

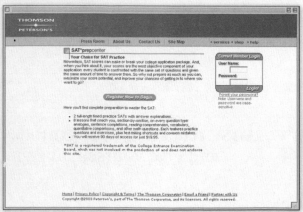

Improve your scores from the comfort of your own computer.

Online Practice Tests for the SAT*, ACT Assessment®, GRE® CAT, GMAT CAT®, TOEFL®, and ASVAB

No matter what test you're taking, the best ways to improve your scores are through repeated practice and a solid understanding of how the test works. Whether you're headed for college, graduate school, or a new career, if your test is computer-adaptive or paper-based, Peterson's online practice tests give you the convenience you crave. Each is completely self-directed. And you get 90 days access so you can log on and off whenever you like. Plus, automated essay question scoring for the GRE, GMAT, and TOEFL!

Visit the Test Preparation Channel of **www.petersons.com**, select your test, and get started.